THE
COMPLETE
HOUSE
INSPECTION
BOOK

THE COMPLETE HOUSE INSPECTION BOOK

(Formerly titled: *The Home Buyer's and Owner's Checklist*)

Don Fredriksson
Illustrated by Rusty van Rossman

Fawcett Columbine • **New York**

A Fawcett Columbine Book
Published by Ballantine Books

Library of Congress Catalog Card Number: 86-92123
ISBN: 0-449-90263-3

Cover design by James R. Harris
Manufactured in the United States of America
First Ballantine Books Edition: February 1988
10 9 8 7 6 5 4 3 2 1

Acknowledgments

George Tretiakoff, master electrician and builder, without whose advice and assistance this book would not have been as complete and accurate. George's substantial contributions to the electrical and structural material covered in this manual have been and are sincerely appreciated.

Douglas Dolan, senior vice president, Victor O. Shinnerer & Company, Inc., insurance executive, who has provided incentive and inspiration to go forward with this comprehensive manual.

Contents

Contents

List of Illustrations

Figure/Description/Page

The Complete House Inspection Checklist

6   A FINAL EXTERIOR EVALUATION

7   EVALUATING SPECIAL INSTALLATIONS

THE
COMPLETE
HOUSE
INSPECTION
BOOK

Introduction

Until recently, the average home buyer and owner had absolutely no idea of the full importance or implications of residential inspection and evaluation. Most folks thought that inspections were the professional concerns of banks, mortgage companies, and the real estate community.

The national trend toward litigation has meant that successful—and litigation-free—real estate transactions have begun to hinge on what is referred to as "disclosure." Disclosure boils down to the seller telling the buyer the complete truth about the structure or piece of property being sold.

The ability to inspect, discover, and evaluate the extent of what are commonly known as "red flag" problems in residential property has therefore become extremely valuable to both potential buyers *and* sellers.

It's obviously a critical skill for home buyers. Even if "full disclosure" is the law of the land, buying a new home is too big an investment to risk making a mistake. Home buyers are beginning to realize that a careful home inspection—either their own or by a professional—is an invaluable tool in protecting themselves from the uncertainties of the house-buying process.

If you know how to thoroughly inspect and evaluate a property, you won't have to depend on the honesty and integrity of people who are trying to sell you something, and you're much more likely not to have to depend on your full-disclosure legal remedies.

If you don't know what to look for, or how to find out what you don't know about a house, you might end up paying too much money for a house riddled with hidden flaws—and paying huge bills just to make it fit to live in.

On the other side of the fence, sellers have to know where and how to look for red-flag problems in order to make proper disclosure for the properties they've put on the market. (A "red flag" is a critical defect which materially lessens the value of a property. If such a defect is not disclosed to a buyer, there is usually cause for legal action on the part of the buyer.)

This book can also help you catch small problems in your own home—before they develop into irreparable damage. Good maintenance habits can prevent costly repairs later, and can even improve your home's resale value.

The information is especially important if you're thinking about selling your home. If your property meets the standards detailed in this book, you should have much less difficulty selling it. The checklist also furnishes a useful blueprint for evaluating the condition of an older residence, and bringing it into good repair.

The essential structural elements, utilities, and appliances that make up a residence are like dominoes stacked front to back. When one falls (or fails), many others can drop. Frayed wiring, for example, can indicate problems—like improper installation or inadequate materials—beyond the surface wear and deterioration. A leaking valve can point to plumbing problems beyond the immediate location, an uneven roofline can be caused by a host of different problems, and stress cracks can indicate much more than a sagging foundation.

If there's one rule that I can't emphasize enough, it's that you should investigate every suspicious discovery that you make. If you can't run it down to its origin, hire a professional to complete the investigation and deliver a conclusive report. You *must* get answers now to avoid getting stuck with costly repairs later.

How to Use This Book

Before you try to use this handy inspection guide, I'd advise you to read it through completely, front to back, to get an idea of the kinds of questions you'll be asking. Preferably, you should read it just before you start inspecting potential properties, so that the information will be fresh in your memory as you walk through them.

Start with the checklist, and decide which items you are most concerned about. Putting a simple check mark in the margin of the master checklist on pages xi–xvii should help you make sure that you don't skip anything important.

If you have a reasonably good memory, referring to the master checklist should be enough to help you recall the important elements you want to cover in each inspection. If not, carry the book with you and use the marked-up checklist as an outline for your inspection, and the expanded text as a reference.

Many of the checklist items include questions that you'll have to ask the seller of, or the agent for, the property you're interested in. Make sure that you take pencil and paper along with you on the inspection, and make notes about both your questions and the answers you receive.

If you want to make absolutely sure that you don't miss anything, take this guide with you and note the answers to your questions in the margins. Whether you use the book or a yellow pad, let the agent or seller see that you're recording the answers to your checklist questions. If you want to double-check your answers, ask the agent or seller to initial and date your notes.

How to Work with a Professional Inspector

A recurring theme throughout this inspection guide is, "When in doubt, call a professional."

These days people are increasingly suspicious of officialdom and so-called experts. The perception is that authority figures of almost every stripe are untrustworthy and unreliable.

This appears to have become a national credo with respect to inspectors of all kinds. Fortunately, based on my experience over the last twenty years, it is my impression that—to the contrary—most professional real estate and construction inspectors are exemplary citizens, good neighbors, and experienced professionals.

There are, of course, bad apples in every shipment, but the overwhelming majority of them are good. Your chances of getting a bad one are about one in sixty. When you finish this book, you should be able to detect that one—if you're unlucky enough to run across him—within minutes.

Inspectors fall into several categories, one or all of which could be encountered by a home buyer in the course of buying a residential property through a real estate broker. They are:

1. The local building inspector
2. The selling real estate broker's inspector
3. The lending institutions's appraiser-inspector
4. The FHA or VA appraiser-inspector
5. The title company inspector-investigator
6. The pest control or termite inspector
7. The buyer's inspector

The *local building inspector* is the person most often encountered in any dealings regulated by local jurisdictions. He can function both as a consumer protection inspector in counties and municipalities where laws and ordinances have been enacted for that purpose and as the official who enforces the various building codes in the district.

If the property under consideration is under renovation during escrow, this inspector could be wearing both of his hats, acting both for the local office and as a consumer protection agent. If you are involved in a renovation during that critical period, you might have to deal with such an inspector.

Which brings me to two other important subjects: working with inspectors and obtaining construction or repair permits, which usually go hand in hand.

The idea of having to get a permit for work on one's own home is repugnant to the average homeowner. The homeowner thinks it implies making detailed mechanical drawings, permitting official snooping, and risking rejection, not to mention paying large fees to bureaucrats who turn up their noses at homeowner applications—as opposed to the submissions of licensed contractors.

Fortunately, in many jurisdictions nothing could be further from the truth. Good public relations are a high priority for almost every politician these days. Many of the high-end bureaucrats serving in local governments are under intense pressure from elected officials—who need public approval to stay in office—to keep their constituents happy.

Today, if you can document your improvement or repair in rough sketches, words, and manufacturer's brochures to the point where the examiner can reasonably determine what you have in mind, you will get your permit. In the great majority of cases the fees are reasonable. Most of them go toward the cost of inspection.

The fact that you are a landowner and a voter, and have taken the trouble to try to comply with the laws on permits puts you ahead of most of the contractors in the neighborhood.

Your inspector should be able to give you very useful hints on your project, so meeting him before you get started and following his advice could make your in-process and final inspections a breeze.

In fact, treating the inspector as a partner in your project can produce a kind of camaraderie that will help you move it along smoothly, and ultimately produce a very good effect "downtown."

Don't be afraid to ask questions or take advice. George Tretiakoff, master electrician and close friend, always asks inspectors for advice the moment they walk on the site of one of his jobs. In almost every instance, he knows the answer before he asks the question, but he keeps quiet and nods as the inspector fills him in on his view of the situation.

From that moment on, George is off on the right foot with his inspector. He gets his final approvals faster than any contractor I've ever met, except me—because I use George's technique, too. It's foolproof.

It's also good practice, because you can always learn something new and important from inspectors. They like to let you know that they're on top of the codes and practices in their specialties, and they're always ready to give you the benefit of their knowledge and experience.

The *selling real estate broker's inspector* is a form of broker's insurance. In almost every case, this inspector is a local licensed building or engineering contractor of recognized reputation who is engaged by the broker to inspect all properties listed by the broker. This inspector will have little or no contact with the buyer, except that the inspection report will probably be included in the escrow with the deposit receipt or escrow instructions.

Naturally, if the buyer later discovers an obvious red-flag error or omission in the inspector's report, and either administrative or legal action is taken on behalf of the buyer, there will probably be contact among all the parties to the transaction. At that time, the buyer's complaints will be examined, and the seller, listing and selling brokers, and inspectors will be closely questioned to determine whether or not fraud or incompetence were involved in the error or omission.

Since the inspection company and the buyer will be in a classic adversarial confrontation, it would be to the buyer's advantage to have the backup of his own inspector, whose role I shall discuss later.

The *lending institution's appraiser-inspector* has the responsibility of protecting the bank's investment. The buyer's loan depends on this inspector's observations and judgment. In a manner of speaking, these people also work for the buyer and may consult with the seller, buyer, and/

or broker during the inspection period. The condition of the neighborhood, local real estate values as they relate to the property in question, the condition of the land and structures, and other matters will be scrutinized in connection with a report to the lender.

The result of this inspection and appraisal will determine the high limit on any contemplated loan on the property.

The *FHA or VA appraiser-inspector*'s job is similar to that of the lender's inspector. These people are either employees of the federal government or contract inspectors hired by the federal government to establish the limits of the government's residential loan guarantees to lending institutions. Quite often these inspectors substitute for those from lenders when FHA or VA loan guarantees are a factor in loan packages.

In most cases, buyers will have little or no contact with these inspectors.

The *title-company inspector-investigator* can also be a contract agent. Very few of them are in-house employees. These people check public and private records on questionable or irregular items discovered during the routine title search procedure. These inspectors are solely concerned with protecting the title company and its insurance policies.

Buyers seldom encounter them except when exceptions or variances to the policy of title insurance to be issued in connection with a transaction are discussed. More often than not, an administrative employee or escrow officer, rather than the inspector of record, will conduct such a conference.

The *pest control or termite inspector* conducts what amounts to a mandatory inspection under most state and local laws in the United States. These people are often the employees of pest control or termite contractors whose job it will be to remedy structural defects or the causes of future structural defects.

The termite inspector is not restricted to reporting on termites and boring pests. These inspections usually cover all manner of structural irregularities, including but not limited to wet and dry rot, foundation displacement, disturbed structural supports of all types, ruptured or displaced siding and flashing seals, insecure or leaking windows and doors—in fact, everything affecting the structural integrity of a residence.

Often the buyer is present when the inspection is made, but it should be noted that, in most cases, the seller or seller's agent has ordered and will pay for the inspection under the terms of the escrow. The inspector's report will therefore be made to the seller or seller's agent for inclusion in the escrow.

Introduction

Disclosure to the buyer will occur at a conference called by the escrow holder or responsible title company officer.

If the buyer is sufficiently knowledgeable, was present during the inspection, and conversed with the inspector about his observations and suggestions, there is a basis for discussing the inspector's report, if the buyer notices any errors or omissions.

It should be emphasized that the buyer has absolutely no right to confer with the inspector prior to the issuance of the report. In fact, most pest control inspectors will refuse to discuss the inspection with anyone but the seller or seller's agent prior to a conference on the report.

This inspection is the second and most important consumer protection inspection. In jurisdictions where the building inspection department is not required to perform a consumer protection inspection, the termite inspector is the buyer's only effective reporter on these matters, despite the fact that he is employed by others.

And then there is your own *buyer's inspector*. More and more often, buyers and those sellers who are anxious to make full disclosure to their brokers and buyers hire professional inspectors to examine and evaluate residential properties.

With the emergence of real estate disclosure laws in some of the more populous states, the increasingly litigious nature of real estate transactions gone wrong, and the ascendance of the consumer protection movement in the United States, the corps of privately hired professional residential inspectors has grown from a few retired building and government inspectors to the American Society for House Inspection (ASHI), with its growing membership and influence on the real estate industry.

In most instances, professional inspectors are licensed building contractors-turned-inspectors, and retired building or government inspectors. Usually, these men and women are qualified by long experience for the job. In a great many jurisdictions they may not be licensed as inspectors by the state or any municipality, because there are no regulatory boards or commissions overseeing the profession at this time. Of course, that will be remedied in due course.

For now, perhaps it would be best to select from among the members of ASHI, and if there are no ASHI accredited inspectors in your area, to apply to your local building department for recommendations from among recently retired building inspectors.

The Yellow Pages of the telephone book now have a category called "Inspection Bureaus," which lists the names of individuals and companies who perform residential inspection services.

When you have selected the individual or agency to inspect a property under consideration, the first thing you should ask is whether or not they have ''errors and omissions insurance.'' If they don't, it's a strike against them. In the states that license inspectors, some require that bonds be posted.

If the selected inspector is ASHI-accredited, a state-licensed inspector, a building contractor, or carries errors and omissions insurance, he or she should be competent and worthy of your trust.

One who doesn't have these rudimentary credentials should be suspect until you have checked references. Of course, I have always taken the position that references are important, even in the cases of credentialed professionals in any classification. Usually, three are sufficient. More are better, and be sure that you check them thoroughly before you hire.

You should be present when the inspection is in progress. Notice if the inspector has a routine that makes sure the examination covers all the critical areas of the structure, from top to bottom or from the bottom up.

The efficient, conscientious inspector will note everything in writing as he comes to it. He won't just look at the attic from a door or access hatch; he'll go through the whole space and note the condition of the wiring and plumbing at the same time as he checks structural items. He should come equipped with ladders to examine the roof closely, and tools to open and check the furnace.

You can usually determine what sort of inspection you'll be getting by the way the inspector presents himself on the job. He should have all the necessary equipment with him and not have to leave to pick up a tool or other items he needs for his inspection.

You should be able to ask relevant questions and get good, solid, understandable answers. Evasive answers, not to the point, are a sign of inexperience and lack of knowledge.

Once you have gone through this book, you should be able to recognize both evasions and incompetence rather quickly.

Your inspector should be able to give you an appraisal of built-in appliances, the plumbing, electrical system, and paving as well as a structural report on every building on the property. The report should be a full and complete written document, suggesting causes and remedies of all noted defects.

When you have received the report, you should show it to the seller, the broker, or the broker's agent and request that it be included in the escrow, for discussion prior to the closing of escrow.

Fees for such inspection services are borne by the buyer alone and can range from a few hundred dollars for a standard three-bedroom residence to a thousand or more for a mansion or estate of larger proportions.

Swimming pool and spa inspections should be handled by a swimming pool/spa contractor or pool maintenance company. They will usually conduct the inspection without charge in hopes of snaring your chemical, equipment, and pool maintenance business later in return for their good offices.

Caveat Emptor

The bottom line is that you've got to look out for your own interests— and in real estate, careful inspection and research are the best ways to make sure that you're getting what you pay for.

In general, read the fine print in any document you sign. Check any information disclosed by the seller and his or her agent against independent sources, if possible. Before you buy, get out your magnifying glass, look at the records, examine the property carefully, check the existing deed, and above all, *ask questions* and *get answers*.

First Steps

Buying a new house is the most expensive—and one of the most complicated—investment decisions that most people will ever get to make. Unfortunately, potential buyers have to analyze an overwhelming amount of information, and some of the most important factors they *should* consider can get overlooked or forgotten.

The list of questions that follows will help you get off on the right foot. The questions will not only help you decide whether a specific neighborhood or house is right for you, but also help you eliminate unsuitable properties from consideration as quickly and efficiently as possible.

Choosing a Neighborhood

Most people select neighborhoods that reflect both their economic resources and their social tastes. These are both important considerations that should give you clear direction in both the kind and location of houses you should look at.

[1] You should be sure that the properties that interest you are within your financial means—and within your ability to provide proper maintenance. You'll find that some neighborhoods are simply out of your price range—while others contain real values. On the other hand, no house is a bargain if rehabilitating and maintaining it will be prohibitively expensive.

[2] Do a little cruising through the neighborhoods that interest you the most. If you're looking for adult living, seeing a great many children riding bikes or hopscotching their way down chalk-marked sidewalks should point you in other directions. Of course, if you have growing children, this kind of neighborhood can be a godsend. Likewise, a retirement

community of sixty- and seventy-year-olds might not fit the tastes of younger adults.

[3] Study the areas you've identified as places where you would like to live. If you don't see any FOR SALE signs in the area, it's possible that everyone who lives there feels the way you do about it, and has dug in to stay.

But it might still be worth visiting your local real estate broker. They may know about a house coming up for sale within a few weeks or months. They might have even received a listing the day before that they haven't posted. Take a chance—you might get lucky.

If you have time, a chat with residents of your target neighborhoods could be an equally valuable guide to the local housing situation.

Regional Considerations

[4] It is also important to know about other geographical, political, or environmental variables that you might need to take into consideration. For example:

[5] If the neighborhood you're considering is located in a forested or agricultural area, are there any plans afoot to carve out new developments? Is the government planning new construction or significant redistricting in the vicinity? Are any new commercial enterprises that might affect the environment in the works?

[6] If you are raising a family, prospective school closings nearby may matter to you. Conversely, plans for a new school building may also be a major consideration.

Answering these questions may require some research. For example, construction on the new school may have run into funding problems, delaying its opening until your little darlings have grown and started families of their own. It's worth thoroughly investigating all important local conditions and restrictions before you decide to buy a house.

Some other regional issues worth looking into:

[7] What kind of people live there? Are they white-collar, blue-collar, professional, laboring, retired, young families, old, established families with few teenage children, adult couples and singles, multifamily dwellers, and so forth?

[8] Check the access to supermarkets, movie theaters, shopping malls, stores and businesses, schools, car services, garbage collection, transportation, and other essential services.

[9] Regional water and sewage services: Are there any special assess-

ments on the sewage or water system, over and above the normal cost of water (for an established or new utility district)? Does the local government plan any change in policy? For instance, does the city plan to ban septic tanks in favor of city sewage service five years down the road?

Evaluating Specific Properties

Once you've found a neighborhood that you like—and possibly, several homes there have caught your eye—here are some of the questions you should ask about specific properties:

[10] Your first concern must be whether or not the house and property you're considering will be at risk from natural causes.

[11] Before you begin your examination of the house and outbuildings, find out what the natural hazards are by talking to the neighbors and checking the city, township, county, or regional records. You might discover that your dreamhouse has flooded every spring for the past five years.

Houses built in particularly hot, cold, damp, or dry areas may require additional protection against the elements. If the residence you wish to examine has been built on exceptionally sandy, rocky, or clay-bearing ground, you should carefully observe what effects, if any, these conditions have had on the building's foundation (figure 1).

[12] Hillside construction is worthy of especially careful inspection (figure 2). If you're looking at a beach house, you should know that salt water, wind, blowing sand, and shifting substrata can all cause special problems. If the property is on a particularly exposed section of the coastline, or in a dike-protected area, flooding can be an ever-present danger.

Next, you can begin to ask more specific questions about the house you're interested in:

[13] How old is the house? How old is the neighborhood?

[14] Is the house on a sewage system, or does it depend on a septic tank? (See [9] above.)

[15] What are the property taxes on the house in question?

[16] What kind—and how much—insulation does the house have—or not have?

[17] What kind of heating system does the house have? Is it natural or liquified-petroleum gas (LPG), oil, coal, solar, recirculating hot water, two-pipe condensing-return steam, single-pipe steam, forced hot air, gravity hot air, hot-water-recirculating radiant heating, electric baseboard, electric radiation, heat pump, and so forth? Try to find out the

Figure 1.

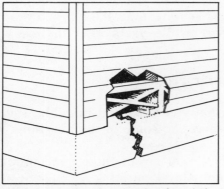
Badly cracked and separating foundation

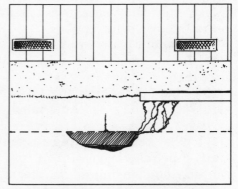
No Concrete Pads

Unsupported porch pilings

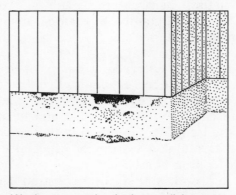
Weak concrete beginning to disintegrate

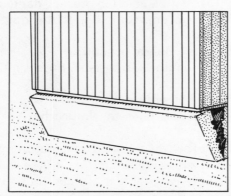
House shift due to sand or shifting substrata. Concrete cracking at centerline

Water undermining foundation due to water puddling at joint of walk or patio and foundation

Figure 2.

Sand

Clay hillside

Rocky hillside

name of the company that services the heating system, and check its condition with them.

[18] What type of hot-water heating is installed? Is it natural or liquified-petroleum gas, oil, electric, solar, or a combination system? What is the system's capacity, and what is its recovery capability? How recently was the system replaced or updated?

[19] If the house is air-conditioned, is it a central system, or are there individual window units? Who maintains the system? Be sure to check with these people before you commit to buy. Air-conditioning systems can be very expensive to repair or replace.

[20] If you object to pets, is the neighborhood pet-ridden? Did the previous owners have pets in the house? This is extremely important to people who have allergies.

[21] If you're still interested in the property after answering these questions, ask your agent if it would be possible to speak with the sellers before you commit to buy—to clarify questions on the house's features that may come up.

Rural Properties

You should ask a similar set of questions about rural properties. As before, the most important considerations are your needs and your priorities. But there are also other concerns that are unique to country real estate:

[22] Rural electrification, or power supply, is an important concern. Investigate the source, availability, and cost of getting power on a property. Perhaps, in time, you'll want to change your land use from dairy pasture to a vineyard, to raising show horses, or even to light industry. Each use has its own power requirements, and you have to make sure—in advance—that adequate electricity is available at reasonable rates.

[23] The water supply is equally important. Does the property depend on well water? Are there additional sources of water—from a utility ditch system, or a government dam? Does the community have a water distribution system that could augment a well? If you are serious about the property, it may be a good idea to suggest that the well be checked for water quality (to detect possible contamination), flow rate, and reserve supply (which is related to the water table level and the depth of the well).

[24] The availability of energy sources, especially natural gas, should be carefully checked. At present, natural gas is the least expensive form

of energy in most parts of the country. In certain circumstances, conversion from electric to natural gas space and water heating may be warranted.

[25] A visit to your local, county, or state agricultural agent could answer all of your questions in one meeting. A few minutes spent with the local installer or maintenance person for the mechanical equipment on a property could give you valuable information about the present condition of these critical items.

The First Visit

If you've managed to get satisfactory answers to most of the preceding questions, and you still think the place is worth a closer look, by all means let the agent or seller show it to you. During this visit, don't ask any further technical questions. Just look at the house and get a feel for it. In many cases you may decide, then and there, to look elsewhere.

If you're convinced that the property is worth pursuing, make a date to see it again a week later—to make your true inspection of the property.

Prepare for this second visit (which I'll cover in detail in Chapter 3) by satisfying yourself that the property meets your most important criteria. Do some preliminary investigating down at the city or county records offices, and meet with local tradespeople or officials who can bring you up-to-date on the current condition of the property.

Don't let an agent try to force you into an earlier date with the old story that someone else is interested in the house and is ready to make a down payment. If it's true, then the best you'll do is give the seller a chance to up the price on the property.

Houses just don't sell that quickly, even in boom times. You'll almost always have a week, and if you don't, you're usually better off walking away from the situation. Look elsewhere. Fine houses come into the market daily, even in the most desirable neighborhoods.

I've heard experienced real estate people say that even if you lose a house you like very much, another is bound to come along that is as good, or better, if you bide your time.

Folks who take their time seldom get ''stung.''

A House Inspection Tool Kit

The Boy Scout motto, *Be prepared,* has always been an excellent rule of thumb—and it's an especially good one to put into practice before you try to inspect a residential property.

To do a truly professional-quality job, you'll need the basic instrument and tool kit shown in figure 3. All of these items are available at hardware stores, building material suppliers, or at an electronics shop. I've listed Radio Shack (Tandy) as the source for one item, but you can probably also obtain an equivalent device elsewhere.

The entire kit should cost under two hundred dollars, and will last for years. Not only will this small investment be worth its weight in gold if it helps you identify the best value in the homes you look at—or avoid houses with expensive hidden problems—but you'll find plenty of use for the tools in property maintenance and repair work.

[26] *Small Carpenter's Try Square.* You use this tool to check whether the walls are square to each other, and to the floors and ceilings. It is also useful for checking the squareness of window and door frames. Cost about seven dollars.

[27] *Stud Finder.* This useful little device will help you find the structural studs behind the walls. All you need do is follow the simple instructions on the package. One inexpensive version is simply a small magnetized post on a pivot, in a plastic bubble. It locates the studs by finding the nails that hold the wallboard in place. They are usually six to eight inches apart, in the studs. Some vertical movement of the instrument will assist you in locating the stud centerlines. A more elaborate type of stud finder is electronic, and is capable of locating any type of structure behind walls. If you can afford the higher cost, the electronic

Figure 3.

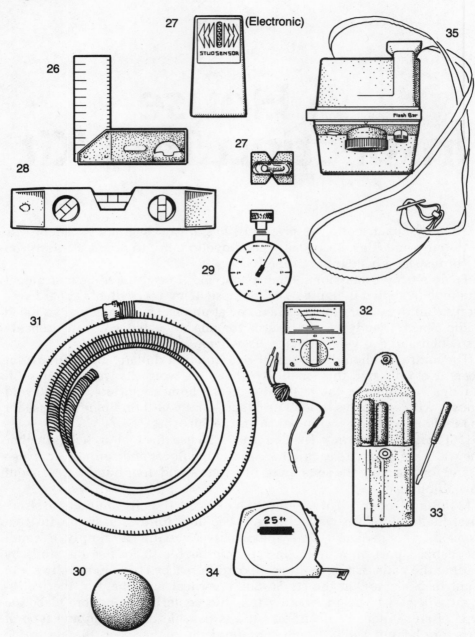

unit would be worth purchasing. Mechanical: cost about five dollars. Electronic: cost about forty dollars.

[28] *Torpedo Level.*   This tool helps you check floor and deck levels. It also helps you to check the "plumb" on walls, to make sure they are perpendicular to foundations. Cost about ten dollars.

[29] *Water Pressure Gauge.*   This is one of the most useful instruments you can buy. Most plumbing supply and building material houses stock it. Insist upon the model that is designed to screw onto the hose threads on a garden valve or hose bibb. Cost about twelve dollars.

[30] *Smooth-Surfaced Rubber Ball.*   This child's toy will be used on concrete decks for a preliminary drainage survey. Cost about $2.50.

[31] *Reel-Type Garden Hose.*   It's best to have the type that rolls up into a compact package. Just keep it in the car trunk. It'll come in mighty handy later for testing for roof leaks and proper drainage. Cost about thirty dollars.

[32] *Microanta Multitester.*   This volt-amp-ohm meter will help you measure and check the electric circuits in the house under consideration. Radio Shack, the manufacturer of this item, has a series of such testers. Choose the least expensive, smallest one. It sells for about ten dollars, and it is adequate for the job intended. You may prefer a simple insulated screwdriver-type continuity and voltage tester. These can be obtained from building materials and hardware stores for less than five dollars.

[33] *Screwdriver Set.*   A plastic kit of several screwdrivers will come in handy to check the conditions inside fixtures, installations, or mechanical devices. Cost about eight dollars.

[34] *Twenty-Five-Foot Measuring Tape.*   It doesn't need to be expensive, but it should be reasonably well made. You'll use this instrument more than any other. Cost about eighteen dollars.

[35] *Polaroid (or other) Instant Camera.*   Make sure the one you get has a flash attachment. You'll use this camera to record the faults and problems you discover during your inspection tours. It should cost about fifty dollars. Remember, a picture is worth a thousand words.

Once you've become proficient in the use of these instruments and tools, and in the way they're used in the tests in this book, you'll be ready to make thorough, diligent, and prudent inspections of residential properties.

First Look: Exterior

Now that you've narrowed your search to a house that you're seriously interested in, it's time to get into the real work of house inspection.

We'll start with a complete first look at the exterior of the house.

These first impressions should play a very important part in your overall evaluation. The condition of the outside structural components, the connections to outside utilities, and the quality of the finish are not only important concerns in their own right, but they're often a good indication of the general quality and upkeep of the house, and a good preparation for what you'll find once you get inside.

[36] When you first approach the property, make a note as to the locations of the water, electric, and gas meters (figure 4). Then begin to note down the following items as you go along:

[37] Are there lawn or other sprinklers in place? Do they work? Where are the control valves? Look at the control valves. Are they the same type as shown in the illustration (figure 6C)? If the sprinkler system doesn't have the protection of special valves like the one in the example, ask the agent whether or not a check valve has been installed on the main sprinkler line to prevent backflow of water from the sprinklers. It is possible for fertilizers and pesticides to get into sprinkler systems, and under certain conditions, this water can backflow into the drinking-water system.

Water Supply

[38] Where does the line from the water meter enter the house? Is there a valve on that line, on the outside of the house? If there isn't, make a note to look for one inside the house. That will be the main house water valve.

Figure 4.

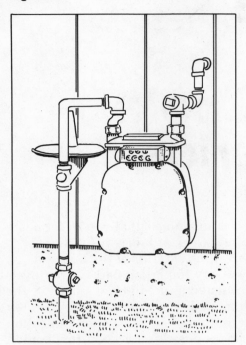

Typical Gas Meter

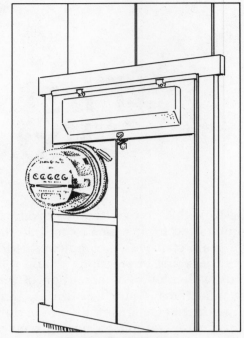

Typical Electric Meter

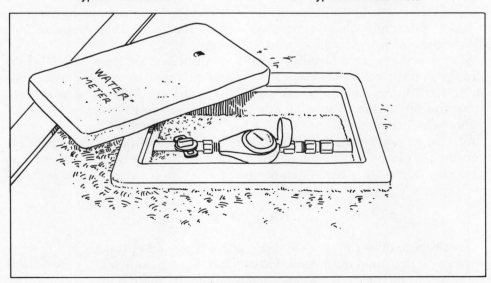

Typical Water Meter

Figure 5.

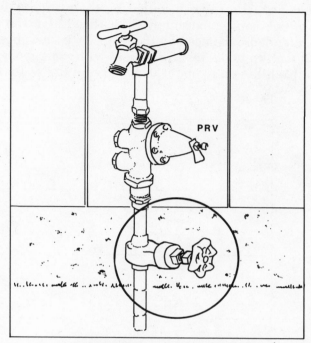

Typical Main House Water Valve
PRV=Typical Water Pressure Regulating Valve

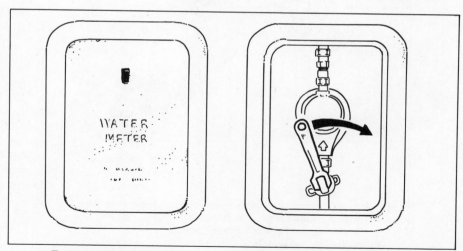

Typical Water Meter Box   Typical Water Meter Main Shutoff Valve

Many houses do not have a main water valve, which means that, in an emergency, the valve installed by the utility at the meter must be shut off, which can be extremely difficult without the proper tools. They are not intended to be used by the property owner (figure 5), which can make it difficult to make repairs or deal with emergency situations.

[39] While you're about it, try to find the water line that takes off from

Figure 6.

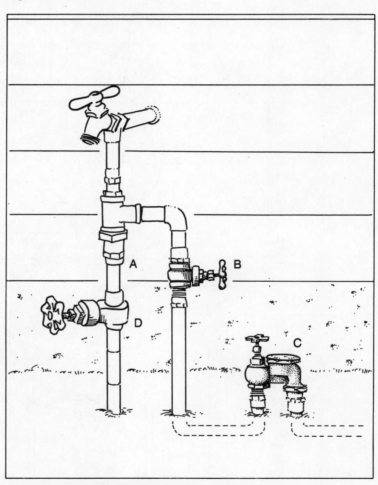

A. Typical Main Water Line from meter
B. Typical Sprinkler Main Shutoff Valve
C. Typical Sprinkler Valve
D. Typical Main House Water Valve

the house water main to the sprinklers. In many cases it is a do-it-yourself weekend job, and may be poorly installed (figure 6).

Electrical Supply

[40] While you're still outside, survey the property's "house-power factor." Modern homes should have a minimum of 100 amperes of 220–240 volts of electricity indicated in the entrance service. It's even better to have 200 amperes at the same voltage level. Many homes being built today have 200-ampere entrance services. The reason is obvious. In the past, houses could get by with 60 amperes of 110–120–volt service because households had relatively fewer appliances and much smaller lighting requirements. Today, with garbage disposers, dishwashers, many electronic gadgets such as multiple television sets, home computers and their peripherals, home workshops, vastly increased lighting requirements, hair dryers, electric skillets, convection, microwave, and electric ovens and stoves, air conditioners, and many more power-hungry appliances, even 100 amperes might be too little.

How can you determine the capacity of a residential electrical system? It's so easy, you'll be surprised when I tell you how it's done (figure 7). First, find the entrance service. The easiest way to do that, with an older home, is to look up and see where the wires come in from the utility pole. You should note whether two or three wires come into the weatherhead fitting on the roof or side of the house. If there are two wires, the house has 110–120 volt power throughout. If there are three, there is 220–240 available at the meter. Next, look at the main circuit breaker or fuse box. In the West, this installation is usually outside the house, just below where the wires come in from the pole. In very cold climates, in the Midwest and East, the main box might be inside, very near where the wires come in from the pole.

Open the box cover and look at the fuses or breakers inside.

If the system has circuit breakers, there is usually a number on the handles of the largest ones. The number can be 60, 70, 80, 90, 100, 150, or 200. Today, it's usually 100. *IMPORTANT: You must look for the biggest breakers, bearing the largest numbers.*

If it is a fuse box, most often the fuses are the cylindrical cartridge snap-in kind, but occasionally you will find plug models that screw in like light bulbs. These plug types are seldom used as main fuses, and are never rated above 30 amperes. Again, look for the cartridge fuses that

27

Figure 7.

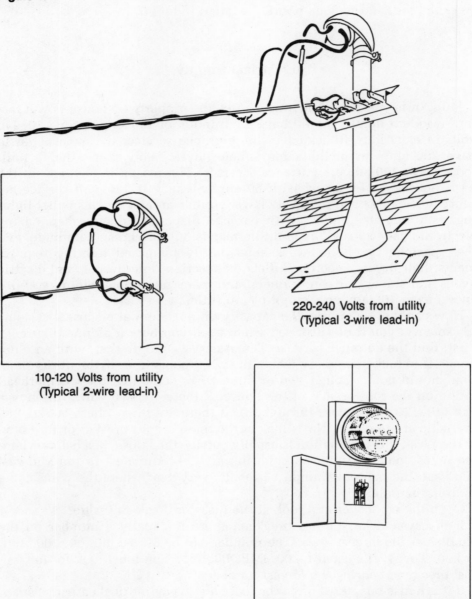

110-120 Volts from utility
(Typical 2-wire lead-in)

220-240 Volts from utility
(Typical 3-wire lead-in)

Typical 220-240 Volt Entrance Service

appear to line up with the incoming main wires, and that bear the highest ratings.

The rating on the highest-numbered fuse or breaker determines the incoming electrical capacity of the house system.

CAUTION: A further note on 115–120–volt, 30-ampere plug fuse boxes. Even though they should not be used as entrance services, some very old urban and rural properties still have them. Quite often, people who are dissatisfied with the constantly blowing fuses that are the result of the insufficient capacity have replaced the fuses with pennies, rendering the *entire wiring system extremely dangerous.*

If the house or property is served by underground utility wires, you may have to undo the faceplate of the breaker panel. Many times you won't have to do that because the wires will be in plain view. A good thing to know, at this point, is that if there are two main breakers joined together at the handles by a small bar, clasp, or pin (figure 8), the house has 220–240–volt service. In a fused service, there will be two of the highest-rated fuses located where the power comes in from the utility. If there is only one, it would be fair to suspect that the system is 110–120.

CAUTION: In many areas of the country, utilities are beginning to eliminate their power poles and are laying all lines beneath the ground. During periods of transition, individual buyers of properties that are located in areas to be converted from overhead to underground power supplies, and whose services require upgrading to achieve full house power, are often forced to pay the full cost of laying the underground service to the utility's connection point or terminal. If this requirement exists on a property you are selling or listing, you *must* disclose it to the buyer. The cost of this upgrading can run thousands of dollars more than the on-premises electrical contract work on the property.

If you are unable to determine the house power of the residence you are inspecting, ask the owner. If he cannot supply the information, call up the utility company. Such data is on record, and can be obtained with minimum delay.

Beware of houses that have 110–120–volt main services. No matter what the ampere rating, the house is underpowered. You must have 220–240 volts for large electrical appliances like stoves, permanently installed electric space-heating equipment, electric water heaters, electric clothes dryers, swimming pool pumps, and air-conditioning equipment.

Beware of houses that have less than 100-ampere capacity for the same reasons.

Note down power deficiencies for later discussion with the seller or for disclosure to potential buyers. (These discussions between buyer and

Figure 8.

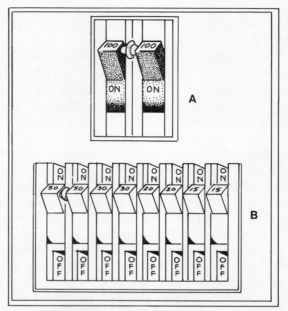

A. Typical 220-240-Volt, 100-Ampere Entrance Service
B. Typical bank of breaker switches

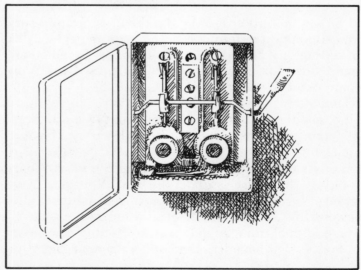

Old-fashioned switchbox with plug-type fuses

seller—or their agents—can lead to remedying problems at the seller's expense, or, if appropriate, at the buyer's expense, with a commensurate lowering of the price of the property, or other valuable consideration.)

Plumbing

[41] Now take another look at the water system where the pipe comes into the house from the meter. First, if you are able to do so from simple observation, determine whether the incoming line is galvanized steel, copper, or plastic. If you are unable to decide from which material the pipe is made by looking at it, just scrape the pipe with a nail file, small penknife blade, or any sharp object, to expose shiny metal. If the metal is silver, the pipe is steel. Of course, copper is reddish gold, and plastic is, usually white or black, and easily recognized.

Next, you want to determine the pipe size. You should realize that the diameter of copper pipe is different from that of galvanized steel and plastic for each pipe size. Don't worry about that. The smaller-diameter copper conducts as much water, size for size, as the relatively larger steel pipes. To assist you in identifying pipe sizes, I suggest that you go to your local plumbing supplier and get some short galvanized or black steel nipples in the size range one-half inch through one and one-quarter inches. At the same time have your supplier cut you six-inch lengths of copper pipe in the same size range. (*Hint:* PVC [plastic] pipe for potable [drinking-quality] water is marketed in steel pipe sizes.) You can use these sample pieces to compare to the pipe on the property you're inspecting.

Most homes have three-quarter-inch main services. A good rule of thumb is that with a water pressure of forty-five pounds or more at the utility main, a three-quarter-inch house main will handle two modern bathrooms, a kitchen, and a laundry without difficulty. A moderate lawn irrigation system can also be tied in without upgrading the main size.

On the other hand, a three-bath home would call for a one-inch house main, as would a house with a large irrigation system or additional water-demanding services. Estates and properties with gate houses, outbuildings, swimming pools, and similar facilities could require sizes larger than one inch.

IMPORTANT: At this point, it is necessary to know exactly how old the house or building is. Carefully investigate the age of any galvanized-steel water system. *Normally, galvanized-steel systems are not replaced with galvanized-steel piping.* For the last thirty-five years, copper has been the material of choice.

Figure 9.

Typical Galvanized Pipe Corrosion
(Tuberculation)

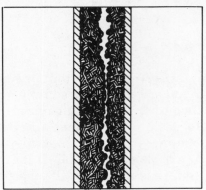

A very low pressure reading

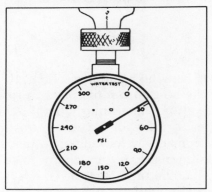

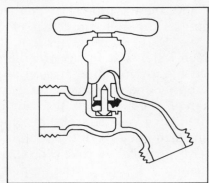

Typical Hose Bibb
with bad washer

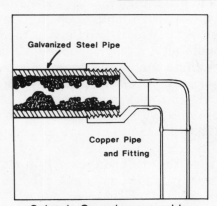

Galvanic Corrosion caused by
connection of dissimilar metals
(zinc-plated steel and copper)

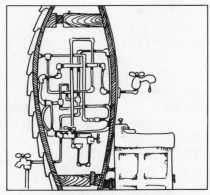

The Handyman's Nightmare
willy-nilly in-wall plumbing

Galvanized-steel pipe is designed for a service life of seventeen years, in normal use. Of course, in areas where corrosion and mineral factors are low, galvanized steel has lasted for the better part of a century. In other locations, steel pipe has been nearly closed by corrosion within fifteen years (figure 9).

Copper and plastic pipes are not subject to the same aging process. Diminished water supply in that piping usually indicates low water pressure at the city mains, or significant mineral build-up, which usually can be remedied by simple treatments. This condition should not be a cause for major concern.

In Chapter 5, I'll show you how to test the water system when you inspect the interior of a house.

Again, note any deficiencies you discover in the water system for later discussion.

Structural Considerations

[42] Now it's time to get an overall impression of the structural condition of the outside of the house. Move back as far away from the house as you can without getting run over by a car in the street. Stand there for a moment and *really look* at the appearance of the house. If the roof is pitched, look carefully at the shingles. Do you see many that are warped or missing? Are the ridge or hip lines smooth (figure 10A), indicating good sealing? If the ridge is shingled, does it look even, with all the shingles spaced the same, and none sticking up or obviously missing (figure 10B)? If you've seriously considering buying the house, I suggest that you photograph the roof from several angles, and look at your snapshots later. Quite often you can pick up irregularities from a picture that you might miss in an on-site inspection. Be especially cautious if you notice a sag in the middle of the ridgeline. This happens frequently in subdivision (tract) homes built in the fifties, especially if they've had more than three layers of roofing applied, without stripping. Four layers of shingles can weigh more than the support structure will bear.

SPECIAL NOTE: In areas where there is danger from brush and forest fires, wooden roofs should be protected by sprinklers. More and more owners in these areas are replacing wood shakes and shingles with metal, vitreous-clay, and concrete tiles.

[43] If the roof is flat (figure 10C), the only test you can make is to apply water, but save that for another day, when you've decided that you're seriously considering the property.

Figure 10.

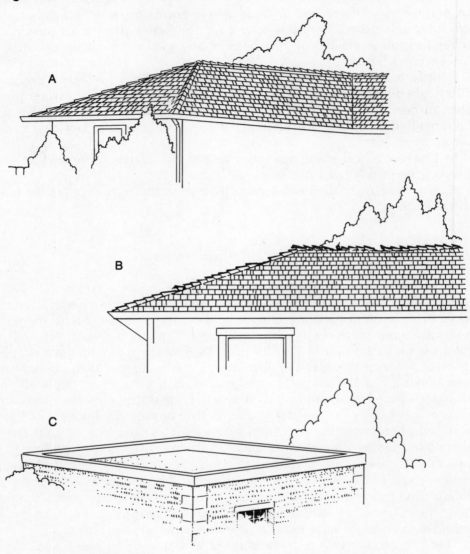

[44] Now notice the roof rainwater gutters at the eaves, if there are any. Do the gutters sag, or are they full of debris? Nearby trees, especially conifers like pine and fir, tend to deposit their needles in house gutter systems. Gutters full of leaves and pine needles (figure 11) will hold moisture for long periods, and are subject to severe rust damage. Just the pres-

Figure 11.

Conifer needles and leaves choking a typical gutter system

ence of trees close to the house is cause for careful examination of the roof and rain disposal system.

For your information, rain gutters are often referred to as "eaves-troughs."

[45] Do the gutters completely span the low, drainage-receiving eaves? Are there large "bananas," or sags, where the supports have either rusted away or have become unfastened? Are the "leaders" or downspouts still serviceable, straight and well secured to the house siding? In Chapter 6 I'll tell you how to determine if the roof rainwater drainage system carries the water to a proper disposal area.

Next, you should take a careful look at the siding. Walk around the house and scan as much of the surface as you can.

Siding Types

[46] Wood siding—Look especially closely on the south side, which usually receives the most sun. Check where surfaces join, where the boards come together, and take note of any large cracks. Notice whether the paint seal is still intact. Try to scrape a small piece of paint away from any obviously weathered area. If a good-size chip comes off, the paint is losing its seal. Also note any painting over badly chipped areas. This is most notable in slapdash paint jobs where the prior paint has not been properly prepared for succeeding coats.

[47] Stress cracks usually appear at corners, around doors and windows, and near foundations. Question any extensive cracking in the framing or siding. It could mean settling foundations.

[48] *Be absolutely sure that all wood surfaces begin at least six inches above ground level. Standard building codes require that no wood be located closer than that to soil, as protection against termites and rot.* If you see wooden siding touching the ground, or coming closer than six inches to it, you'll have to have a full termite inspection done by a licensed termite (pest control) contractor, to make sure that there is no damage.

All reputable builders observe the six-inch siding clearance rule, whether it is code in your area or not. It's just common sense. In the case of an older home or building, combinations of soil and vegetation may have built up around the foundations over the years, causing the wooden siding to become embedded in these materials. This is especially hazardous, because this destructive "mulch" holds a great deal of water, and can cause extensive siding rot. Whatever happens, the siding *must* be cleared from any contact with the soil, *quickly*.

SPECIAL NOTE: Some jurisdictions require twelve inches of clearance between wood and the soil. Check with the local building department to determine the proper clearance for your area.

[49] Shingle siding—Treat wooden shingles exactly as you would any other wood siding. The same precautions must be observed, including that the shingles must terminate at least six inches above the soil. Between the dirt and the bottom line of shingles, you should see only the foundations.

[50] Now look at the shingles themselves. Are they evenly placed and overlapping uniformly? Do they show signs of profound deterioration (figure 12)? Are they warped badly? Do they finish neatly at the corners, around the windows and doors, and under the eaves? Are they all intact, or do you see some splitting or in the advanced stages of rotting? Appearance is *always* a good indication of condition. If the shingles look ragged, split, warped, uneven, or rounded about the edges (from deterioration), chances are that a reshingling job will probably be necessary in the short term. Properly sealed or stained shingles usually last much longer than untreated ones. Cedar shingles are the best. You can identify them by their color (darker than pine or fir, and often reddish, or streaked with a reddish tinge, along the grain).

Composition shingles are less susceptible to damage from contact with the soil, but the code still requires that all siding, of whatever type, terminate six inches above grade. The reason is quite simple. Usually, there is a wooden support structure (framing) beneath the siding. With the siding in contact with the soil, under certain circumstances water can be "sucked" up between the siding and the framing, thus affecting the framing itself.

Walk over and gently lift one of the shingles from the lower edge. You can do this only with a composition shingle of the asphalt or plastic variety. Metal and wooden shingles will resist any attempts to curl them back upon themselves.

If the shingle you lift seems to be brittle, let it fall back into place, naturally. If you are not careful with weathered, brittle shingles, they will crack, and if you apply any further bending tension to them, they will break.

A brittle composition or plastic shingle is evidence of protracted service and weathering. It is another indication to be noted carefully, because it is a portent of possible material failure—and expensive replacement—in the not too distant future.

Figure 12.

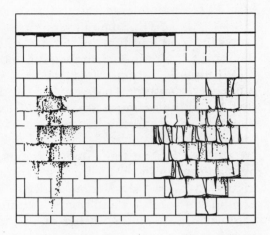

Typical examples of deteriorating or poorly installed Shingle Siding

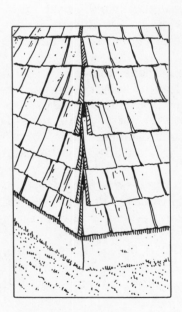

[51] CAUTION: Recently a new kind of plastic shingle has been appearing on the market. Some brands are imported, and others are of domestic manufacture. These shingles are fabricated of a combination of reground used car tires, polyethylene, and a fiber or granular additive, ranging from sand to old, shredded rug fibers. This material has proven to be more durable and weather-resistant than any other composition material tried so far. These products are, however, quite rigid, and will not bend easily. Keep that in mind when you test siding materials for weathering and deterioration. The new material is easy to identify. It is almost always thicker than conventional shingling, and it has a somewhat granular, yet waxy-smooth texture on the underside.

The thinner asphalt-based and light plastic materials, which I mentioned before, will not resist your attempts to bend them. If they are going bad, they will give signs of cracking or breaking. The new, thicker product won't even allow the attempted flexing.

[52] If the shingles are metallic, usually aluminum or plated steel, make sure that the paint bonds are intact. Some of these shingles are coated with a bonded finish. Others are painted after they are installed, and should be repainted regularly to preserve their appearance and keep them from deteriorating.

Aluminum shingles are particularly susceptible to attack by salt air, so if the house is located near the ocean or any large body of salt water, the siding should be checked regularly. The same goes for houses situated in heavy snow areas where the roads are treated with rock salt in the winter.

[53] Metal siding—A variety of metal products have been used as siding over the past hundred years. Most of them are steel, coated with many different rust-resisting products, from zinc (galvanizing) and bituminous emulsions (tar) to tin and cadmium. Coated metal siding has to be painted as well for maximum protection.

[54] Check the integrity of all painted steel siding. Look for any large scratches or dents that have breached the outer paint, and which affect the basic coating beneath. Scratches and dents to bare metal will quickly rust and eventually oxidize much of the adjoining area. Any evidence of rust on siding must eventually be removed and all coating breaches repaired. Take careful note of nailheads surrounded by a halo of rust, or that are totally rusted out.

[55] There are several different types of masonry walls and façades, including cinder block, brick, fieldstone, and poured concrete, both pre-stressed and reinforced. Most of these are fairly impervious to attacks by the elements. Again, appearance is everything. Any obvious deteriora-

Figure 13.

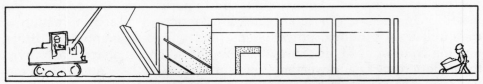

Usual methods of Tilt-up Concrete Wall Construction

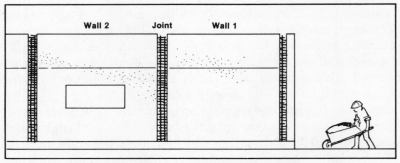

Tilt-up Concrete Wall Construction

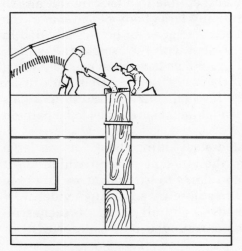

Pouring concrete at joint

Joint weeping water during rainstorm
due to lack of waterproofing

tion, crumbling, cracking, separation of surfaces, settling, or the appearance of wetness over a significant area is grounds for further inquiry.

[56] Far and away the most durable construction material is properly proportioned, well-poured and compacted reinforced concrete. All concrete surfaces must either be laid on waterproof membranes or be adequately treated to prevent any water penetration from the outside. Usually, concrete walls are plastered or brick-veneered on the outside for decorative effect. Care must be taken to determine exactly what type of concrete construction has been used. A fully poured reinforced-concrete house is quite different from a poured slab with tilt-up prefabricated wall sections. The latter has built-in problems in that all of the joints had to be concreted after the walls were erected (figure 13). Bad-mix pours, improperly tamped or vibrated, can reduce structural integrity where walls and corners join. Those are also the very places where leaks can and do occur. "Wet strips," rectangular, uniformly configured, and several inches to several feet wide, are indicators of poured structural pilasters or joint gaps that don't prevent water intrusion from roof surfaces or driven rain. Some of these areas act as wicks and draw moisture from the earth.

Peeling painted surfaces, jagged fallen-plaster patches, missing façade bricks or veneer stones, and obvious crack patterns are signs of trouble.

[57] Brick and cinder block construction generally fall into the same category. Cinder blocks are just oversize bricks, but with one notable exception. If properly installed, they are nearly as strong and durable as poured reinforced concrete.

Brick is considered to be a weaker construction material, but if well laid by competent journeyman masons, it is among the most durable building materials known to man.

Usually both materials are left in their natural state, unpainted or unplastered. To be properly installed, however, both of them must be sealed against the elements. Usually, the inside surfaces are faced with either sheetrock or paneling. Quite often, however, the pleasing appearance of brick or cinder block is left uncovered. Again, the important consideration is waterproofing. Look for it on the outside as well as on the interior surfaces. Quite often, roof runoff leaves telltale wet staining on cinder block and brick surfaces.

A brick or decorative stone façade, or paint on cinder block or concrete surfaces, can give valuable clues as to the water resistance of the structure itself (see figure 14). Blistering, peeling, or missing pieces are cause for concern.

The same basic rules apply to the examination of all masonry surfaces. They must be waterproof and give no evidence of "wicking" (sucking

Figure 14.

Brick (masonry) cracks in critical places

water from the ground). All decorative applications must be in good condition and unbroken.

Brick and cinder block mortar (the binding plaster between the brick or block surfaces) must be sound and without noticeable gaps, powdering, or fractures.

[58] Stucco and veneer facades not affixed to concrete or cinder block outer walls follow the same rules as wooden siding construction. After all, they are both laid on wood framing. Generally, they must follow the "six-inch rule," because of the possibility of wicking. If the stucco or masonry façade touches the ground, it can bring up water into the wood framing. Rot can follow, along with the possibility of invasions by colonies of termites.

Take special note of spiderweb-type cracking on stucco surfaces. A weblike lattice of fine cracks is an almost certain indication of dry rot in the wood on which the stucco has been installed. These irregular and circular cracks are often patched and painted over, but they can usually be detected by a careful inspector. Textural changes and raised patches should trigger your suspicions. The problem may require very expensive reconstruction work.

Veneers can be made of many materials, including fieldstone, flagstone, red brick, yellow brick, decorative concrete resembling stone, and tile.

Examine these siding materials carefully. Look for patched areas and missing veneer components. If you are in doubt about the cause or history of a problem you notice, ask the agent or the seller, presumably the owner, as well.

[59] Foundation vents are *musts* in all wood frame construction. They must also be installed in certain types of masonry structures. These vents appear just above the foundations, on the outside of the house. They are almost always rectangular, made of galvanized steel, often painted over, and are screened or louvered. One type is four by twelve inches. Others go from that size up to six by eighteen inches. Often you will find them hidden behind bushes and flowers. They should occur fairly frequently all the way around the house.

Where there are foundation vents there is usually a crawl space beneath the house. In most states the various codes specify the vertical height of that space as thirty inches or more. Usually the under-house–space floor is lower than the outside grade, exposing more of the foundation and making it easier to examine for cracks and other foundation damage. (Please refer to figure 1.)

As with everything in life, there are exceptions to the "foundation vent rule." Some types of slab-on-grade structures are exempt from the need for foundation vents because the slab of concrete that forms the entire floor of the house *and* the foundations are monolithic (one solid piece). There is no space beneath the first floor to vent. This building technique is not permitted any longer in some jurisdictions.

If there are no foundation vents on a stucco house, look up toward the roof and see if there are vents beneath the overhang of a flat roof. If you see them, you should realize that they are substitutes for foundation vents on slab-based stucco houses.

If you see no vents at all, make inquiries. The *only* types of houses designed without mandatory foundation vents and/or high vents are slab-on-grade nonstucco structures.

Depending on state or local codes, you could find two kinds of membranes in crawl spaces: (1) a vapor barrier, consisting of plastic sheets laid directly on the earth, and (2) rat-proofing, which is simply a relatively thin conforming pour or spray (Gunite) of concrete. It's not slab thickness, but rather an impervious barrier to burrowing rodents. Rat-proofing concrete should not crack or break beneath your body weight. It

43

also acts as a kind of vapor barrier. The best of both worlds is concrete on plastic. Either or both is desirable and, in some locales, required by code.

Trim

[60] Now it's important to look at the trim and flashing. Trim finishes the edges at corners and around windows and doors. It should be properly installed and intact. Quite often it is made of the same material as the siding, but alternative products can be substituted. As an example, a wooden-sided house could be trimmed with aluminum, as could a composition shingle house. Plastic and composition trim have been used with all siding materials (figure 15).

In some jurisdictions, the code requires an extra rain flashing over each exterior door and window. This flashing is simply a piece of sheet metal bent at right angles. One flange of the piece is nailed under the siding, and the other stands out from the house to deflect any water that is running down the siding, away from the window or door. They are great rot preventers and furnish another barrier against water penetration of the casings.

Flashing is most often made of aluminum or steel. It can also be fabricated from plastic or lead. You will find it where pipes and flues come through the roof and sides of the house. It is also used to form the waterproof seal around chimneys and vents on the roof. Some structures are flashed between the siding and foundations. Faulty, cracked, warped, and dislocated flashing can be the cause of over fifty percent of the leaks in an otherwise apparently sound house. I used the word "apparently" because occasionally a sound-appearing structure has hidden faults that only show up after it has been occupied through all four seasons.

[61] Take special care to look at the doors, door casings, window glass, and sash (figure 16). If the panes are puttied to the frames, note the condition of the putty. Sometimes buyers will fuss over any number of trivial perceived faults, but ignore a primary one. If the putty is cracked, or in some places completely missing, you have a problem, which should be the first order of business if and when you take possession.

[62] Look closely at outside stairs, porches, decks, and railings. Most often, only the wooden variety are a problem; however, metal railings and concrete surfaces can go bad and should be scrutinized. Wooden stairs should be tested for excessive springiness, especially in the middle of the tread. The face board of the lowest step should not be touching the

Figure 15.

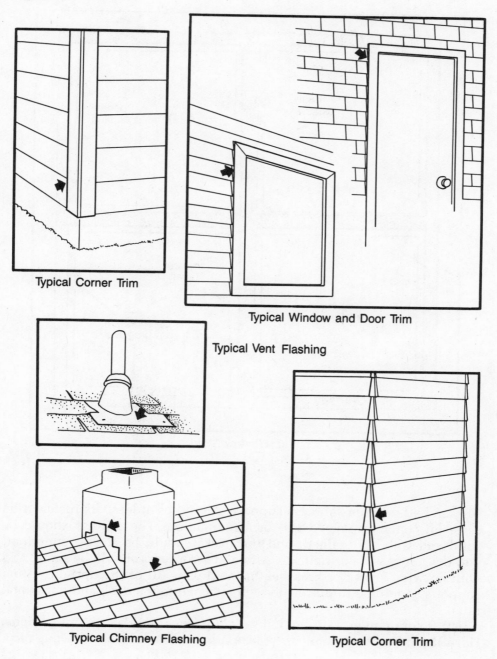

Typical Corner Trim

Typical Window and Door Trim

Typical Vent Flashing

Typical Chimney Flashing

Typical Corner Trim

Figure 16.

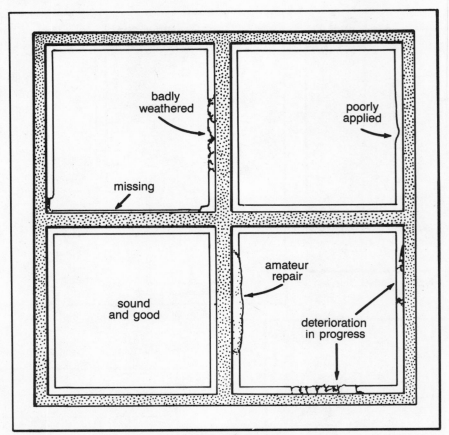

The Window Story

soil, and all wooden staircase supports should be at least six inches from earth on concrete piers, pads, or a foundation. The railings should be solid and well maintained, and the decks should be steady underfoot, without noticeable springiness. All painted surfaces should be sound and without wide cracks or breaches in the finish. All of the upright railing supports should be in place and well attached to the deck and horizontal rails.

[63] Before you go into the house, glance over the lawns and gardens. Have the lawns been kept up? Make allowances for lack of occupancy,

although most conscientious sellers will make arrangements for maintenance of the property in their absence. If the house is occupied by the seller or renters, you can easily determine the level of maintenance by the condition of the outside and garden, which is usually a good indication of pride of ownership and general care.

First Look: Interior

Now that you've taken a long, hard look at the outside of the house, it's time to take a first look inside. At this point, you'll just want to make a quick tour through the house to see whether you like the general layout and construction. Later, if you're still interested in the house, you'll return to make a more thorough examination of the heating, electrical, plumbing, and structural characteristics of the house. (This inspection is covered in detail in Chapter 5).

[64] The first thing you should notice is the way the front door opens. Does it stick slightly? Do the locks and bolts work smoothly and well? Is the door excessively weathered? Is there weatherstripping around the door? If so, is it intact? If you enter through another door, look for the same qualities and conditions.

[65] *All outer doors must be solid-core doors* (figure 17). This is code in most states. You can tell solid-core doors simply by rapping on them with your knuckles. If there is a hollow, drumlike sound, the door is hollow-core, and very unsafe against attempted violent entry. The solid-core door feels and sounds heavy and solid. The lock sets should be in good condition, and every outer door should have a dead bolt. Doors with large areas of light, single-strength glass should be replaced with stronger, less vulnerable doors, as soon as possible.

The test for weatherstripping is basic. Simply open and close the door a couple of times. You can feel the seal take hold as soon as the door moves into its frame. If it is daylight outside, step back into the entry-way and look at the door. There should be no light showing where the door meets its frame. If you see a rectangular halo of light around the door, there is no seal at all.

Figure 17.

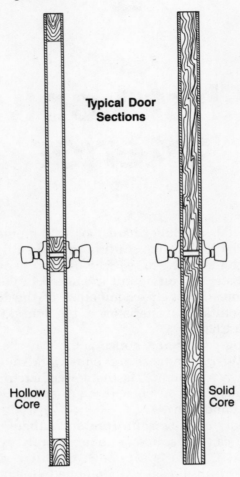

Typical Door
Sections

Hollow
Core

Solid
Core

At this point, it should be mentioned that it is preferable to make your first major inspection during the daylight hours, the sunnier the better. Apart from the obvious reasons, the electricity might be off, making a night inspection possible only by flashlight or portable lantern. That would be tantamount to a blind person playing poker.

First Look: Interior

Layout

[66] Now you should begin a walk-through tour of the interior. A simple examination of the layout of the house is your first priority. Don't attempt to test anything. What you want to know is if the house's spaces are suitable to your needs (figure 18). The best place to start is from the main entry, the front door or vestibule. That is the way guests will see it when they visit. Even if you enter the house from another door, start your inspection from the street entrance.

[67] As you walk through the house, notice the access patterns to each major area. Most people are put off by plans that take them from the main entrance into the kitchen and dining areas, through corridors onto which the bedrooms open. It is usually best for the bedrooms to have a low-traffic area to themselves, and be separated from the entertainment and work spaces of the home.

[68] Everyone has some idea of what a kitchen *should* be. Recently, people have rediscovered the American kitchen, which was at one time the center of the home. A good-size room, allowing for large appliances and a breakfast table, is most in demand. Other folks prefer a compact food-preparation area, and a dining room for all meals. One thing is sure, however: the kitchen should be light and airy, and look out on a pleasant panorama, such as a garden or other soothing natural vista. A south-facing kitchen is ideal. This is usually the busiest and most important room in the home. If the kitchen is inconveniently configured or very dark during the daylight hours you will need to decide if you can live with the arrangement.

[69] While in the kitchen, look for the laundry room or facilities. Because of the plumbing requirements, this important area is usually located near the kitchen or bathroom(s). It is counterproductive to have the laundry facilities in the kitchen. Quite aside from the noise and space requirements, there is the additional heat introduced into the room by the clothes dryer. The ideal arrangement is a separate laundry room, or a laundry in a basement area.

[70] The locations of the bathrooms are also critical. Normally, in a two-bathroom or larger home, one is adjacent to the master bedroom, and the other(s) is/are easily accessible from the other sleeping rooms. Sometimes, a third "half bath" or water closet is located near the kitchen. In two-bath and larger plans, it is ideal to have full bath and shower facilities in each bathroom. These days, however, most plans include one full bath—with shower—in the master suite, and shower-only bathrooms serv-

51

Figure 18.

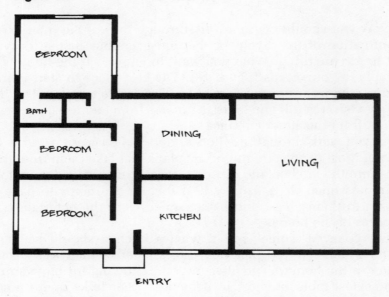

Typical poor plan

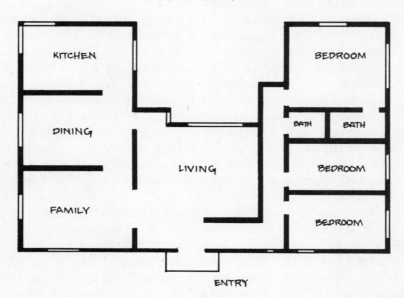

Typical acceptable plan

ing the balance of the bedrooms, and for guest use. Naturally, each bathroom should have a lavatory (hand basin) and water closet (toilet).

NOTE: Some codes prohibit a bathroom or toilet opening directly off a kitchen. In those areas, there must be two doors between the two rooms.

[71] As you're walking around the house, notice the amount of give and springiness to the floors. Loud creaks and other noises should be looked into later on, if you decide you like the house. At the same time take casual note of any significant wall cracking and separation, as well as the condition of the ceilings.

[72] The layout of the sleeping rooms is important. Generally speaking, they should be in the rear of the house, away from street noise. They should have sufficient windows to admit plenty of daylight. (Dark bedrooms can become quite depressing.) Another factor of importance is window size and distances from the floor to the sills. In case of fire, children have a difficult time getting out of windows set too high off the floors. Window closure mechanisms are also important from that point of view. Windows should open easily from the inside, yet be reasonably burglarproof. They should also open sufficiently wide to permit escape in case of fire.

[73] Closets and storge space are primary concerns. In modern homes, closets are usually walk-ins, or are very spacious sliding-door types. Other storage spaces in attics, basements, and cellars should meet the needs of your family. Very often it happens that kitchen cabinets, linen storage, clothes closets, and other cabinets are fine, but when the new owners move in, they find that the "overflow" storage facilities are totally inadequate for the collection of "rare junk" that they've hauled from one house or apartment to the next. If they're determined to keep that collection, obviously they'll need places to store it. Now is the time to consider where that will be. If you can't see sufficient space in the existing structures, you'll have to make another investment in building after the sale.

[74] If you like what you've seen when you've completed your inside tour, make a date to return to the house for a complete examination of the interior. If the seller insists that whatever further inspection you contemplate must be done at that time, you can begin the detailed examination described in the following chapter on the spot.

A Complete Interior Inspection

Before you undertake this detailed interior inspection, which will probably take the better part of three hours, you should be satisfied that the property sufficiently interests you to be worth the additional time.

The main reason for such a close look is to evaluate the cost of bringing the property into first-class, code-satisfactory condition. It is also helpful when comparing it with other similar properties. If you think about it, two nearly identical houses can end up costing considerably different prices. There's an obvious disparity in value between a one-hundred-thousand-dollar house with nothing that needs to be upgraded or repaired versus a similarly priced property that requires a twenty-thousand-dollar investment the moment escrow closes.

The initial tests should be applied to the utilities, because they are the best indicators of the property's overall condition.

Water Supply Plumbing

You can make the following tests only if the water is turned on. I consider the plumbing tests that follow to be some of the more important in this book. If you are serious about the property, you should arrange for the house water to be on when you make your inspection.

[75] Starting in the kitchen, open both the hot- and cold-water faucets halfway (figure 19). If there is a single-handle fixture, place the handle in the middle (temperature) and lift it to about the middle of the interval between full open and full closed. If there is a very small stream, remove the aerator. The aerator is the small chrome or brass tip on the spout that

Figure 19.

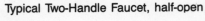

Typical Two-Handle Faucet, half-open

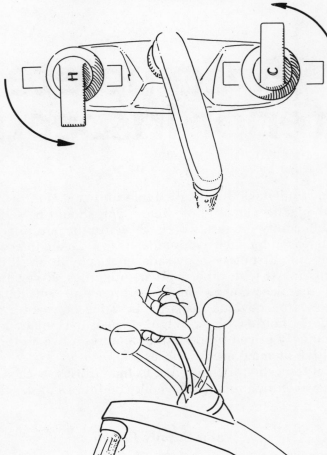

Typical Mono-Handle Faucet, half-open

breaks up the stream and mixes air with the water for a nonsplash, soft-flowing discharge. Sometimes this fitting fills with silt and other debris, restricting the flow. You can eliminate the problem simply by turning out the tip with an ordinary pair of pliers. The fitting should screw off fairly easily.

If the first water that comes out of the spout is red with rust, chances are that the house is plumbed with galvanized-steel pipe throughout, and that the water system is badly corroded. Red water is a warning sign of potential trouble that could require replacement of the entire water supply system in the not too distant future.

If you see a black residue coming out with the first water out of the tap, check the hot-water side by turning off the cold-water faucet, or by moving the mono-handle all the way to the left. If the black gets darker, you're getting another kind of warning. That sediment could be coming out of the water heater. The heating element or burner is probably off, in which case the water will be cold. The discharge of black sediment is an indication that the water heater might require purging. (Purging is a simple do-it-yourself procedure consisting mainly of turning off the cold water supply to the heater, opening the hot water taps in the house, and draining the heater's contents. If the heater will not drain, call a plumber.)

The black coloration could also be coming from the city main water supply. If, upon examination (see page 63), you find the heater to be in acceptable condition, call the local water utility and ask for a water analysis.

[76] Now open the valves on each tub, shower, lavatory (hand basin), and stationary (laundry) tub. CAUTION: Bathtub fillers of some types discharge large quantities of water. In order to conduct a fair test, open the filler valves just enough to make a good flow, or better yet, turn on the shower valves only. That way you won't be overloading the system.

[77] With all of the faucets open, the house's water system should permit all of the fixtures to operate at a fair rate of discharge. If you find one of them to be "starving" for water, with a very low flow rate, either the water supply system has begun to corrode and clog, or the pipe sizes and/ or delivery pressure are inadequate. The Uniform Plumbing Code sizes pipes to permit all fixtures to be operated simultaneously. To isolate the problem, turn all but the slow-running fixtures off. If they discharge good, full streams of water, the water system is out of balance hydraulically. If they continue to flow slowly, it could mean that those particular fixtures will need attention, but that the overall water system pipe network could be in good operating condition.

SPECIAL NOTE: If there is generally sluggish water flow, it would be a good idea to measure the system's water pressure. Take your WATER PRESSURE GAUGE and screw it onto one of the garden valves (hose bibbs) outside. Turn all other faucets off. Turn on the water at the hose bibb. The gauge will read the static water pressure of the city mains at the house. If it is less than twenty-five-pounds per square inch, reconcile yourself to slow-running plumbing fixtures. You will be severely restricted in the number of taps that can be open at one time in bathrooms, service areas, and the kitchen. You will probably have nearly no house water pressure when the lawn sprinklers are in operation.

Low water pressure can be professionally remedied by installing in-line booster pumps, which require the written permission of the utility company. Another way to go is the upgrading in size of all of the pipe in the water system, which can cost an arm and a leg. It is the same as replumbing the entire house, from the meter to the top bathroom in the building.

If your initial outside inspection has revealed that the house is plumbed in galvanized-steel pipe, ask the owners if the interior plumbing is also galvanized-steel pipe. If their answer is, "It was, but we've replumbed the interior with copper pipe," you'll have a new set of questions about the presence of low water flow. Those will have to be answered by a licensed master plumber (plumbing contractor), or, perhaps, by you, if through experience or extensive study you are qualified to evaluate the plumbing system.

Suffice to say that the causes of such poor performance can be any of the following, as well as others too technical to describe here (see figure 9).

1. Badly corroded galvanized-steel pipe
2. Low water delivery pressure either from the utility or the well pump
3. Faulty faucets, or valves
4. Galvanic corrosion—where steel pipe joins copper pipe—in replaced piping
5. A do-it-yourself project wherein the owner-builder failed to consider the hydraulics of his modifications

If extensive replumbing is required to bring the water system up to full function, the cost can range from considerable to prohibitive.

[78] As you close the faucets, stopping the water flow at each fixture, do not shut them off too forcefully. You want to test each of them for drips. Water valves, hose bibbs, and sink faucets are not meant to be closed so tightly that you have to grunt with the effort. They should shut off and be drip-proof with a simple twist of the wrist. If you find one that continues to run or drip, apply just a bit more force to the handle. If it stops then, make a mental note of the fixture, and earmark it for further inspection later. If even this additional force fails to eliminate the flow or drip, the faucet will need close examination and possible replacement of parts. Ask the owners about the history of the unit in question. At the

same time, find out if and when faucet washers or the valve kits in washerless faucets had been checked or replaced.

[79] The fill-spouts on the bathtubs and the shower heads will take a bit of time to stop their flow, so after you've closed their valves, continue on with your inspection. Come back about five minutes later and see if they have stopped dripping. If there is still flow or drips, they'll need attention later.

[80] When you are looking beneath fixtures such as the kitchen sink, a lavatory (bathroom basin), or a toilet, take note of the pipes coming out of the wall. In most cases, you will be able to determine the type of pipe used for the inside plumbing from what's coming through the wall. If you see copper pipe (which you learned to identify on page 31), chances are that the house is plumbed in copper. If you see galvanized pipe coming out of the wall, it is a good bet that the rest of the pipe is galvanized steel. However, many plumbers have plumbed houses in copper but used galvanized-steel nipples (short lengths of threaded pipe) to make connections to fixtures through walls. The rule here is that if you see copper, it's over ninety percent certain that all of the water supply plumbing is copper (figure 20). But if you see galvanized steel and the owners insist that the house was plumbed in copper during their residency, you can either accept their word or make a note to verify their statement. (A good way to do that is to ask the name of the master plumber [plumbing contractor] who did the work.) Keep in mind that those galvanized-steel nipples must eventually be replaced with red-brass ones to keep the system from deteriorating from galvanic corrosion. If it's a do-it-yourself project, ask the owners to show you some of their pipe runs. The best place to check these is at the house water heater (see [82]).

[81] Chrome-plated or plain brass angle stops or valves should be in place beneath each fixture in the house, except showers and bathtubs (figure 21). If they are missing from any fixture, it should be so noted. Not only are they required by the code, but they are designed to make servicing faucets easier.

[82] The water heater is another "weather vane" appliance. A great deal can be determined about the house's maintenance from the condition and environment of the heater. A few things are important to know. Current codes require that a natural gas (or LPG), oil, or coal-fired water heater must be mounted on a platform eighteen inches above the floor level of a residential garage (figure 22). This regulation applies to water heaters that are not in a separate enclosure with a door. The reason for the regulation is simple and very reasonable. Automobile gasoline vapors are heavier than air. If your car has a leaking gas tank, or the tank cap does not

Figure 20.

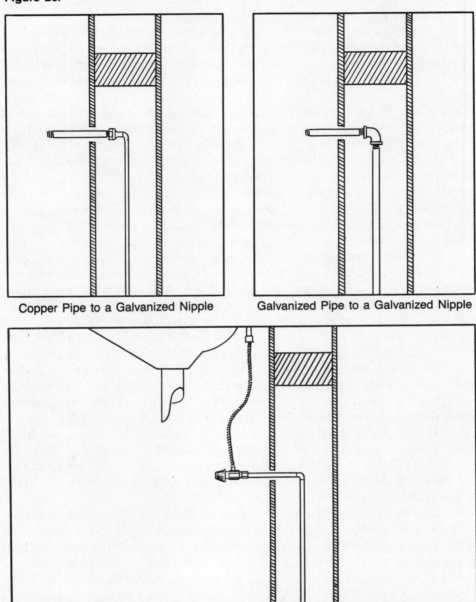

Copper Pipe to a Galvanized Nipple   Galvanized Pipe to a Galvanized Nipple

Copper Pipe to a Copper Nipple

Figure 21.

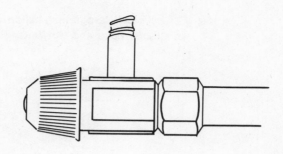

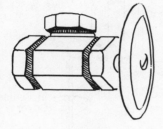

Angle Stops

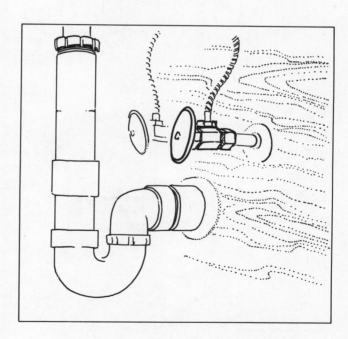

Figure 22.

**Typical Garage Installation
of Gas Furnace and Hot-Water Heater**

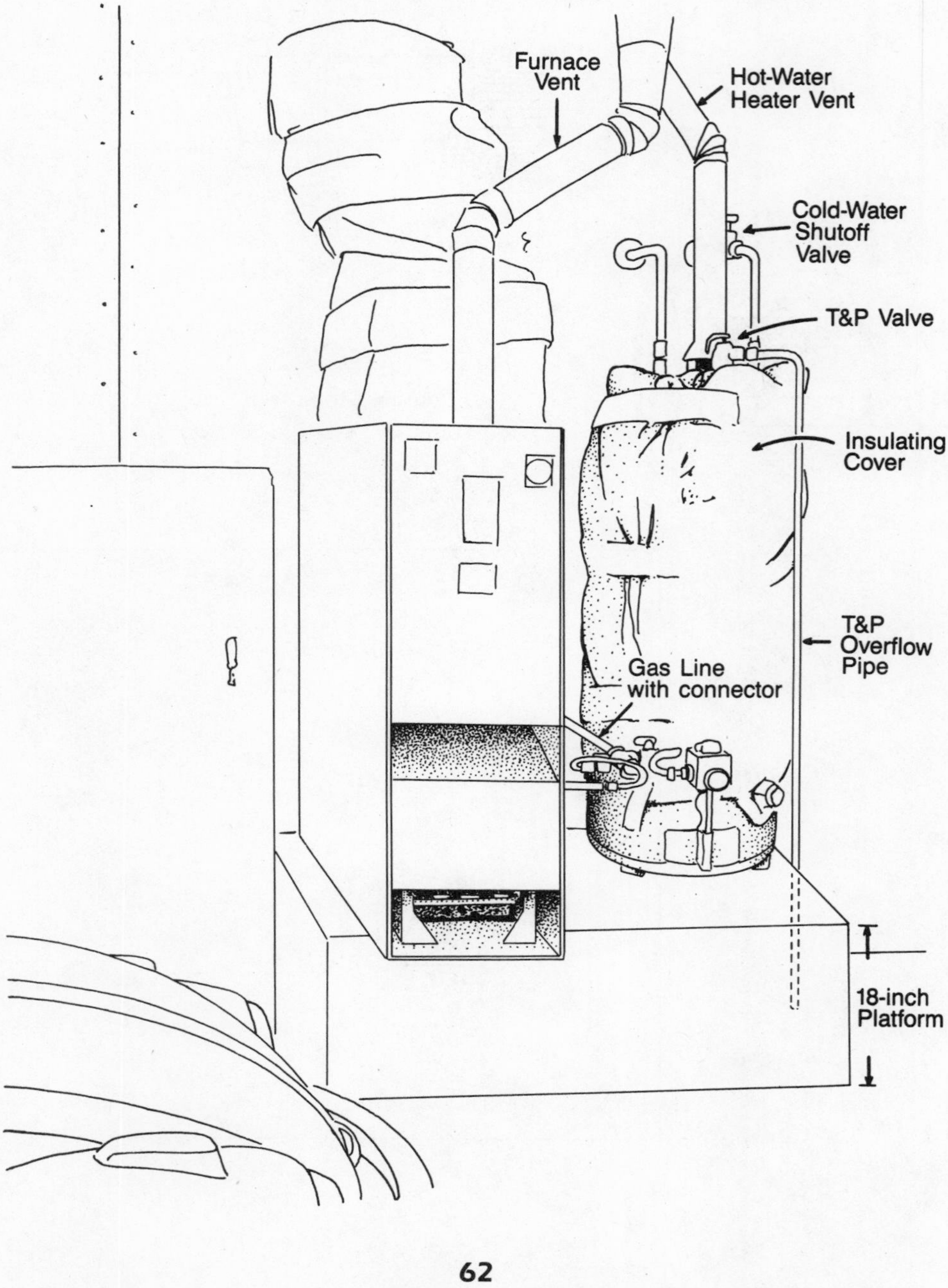

Furnace
Vent

Hot-Water
Heater Vent

Cold-Water
Shutoff
Valve

T&P Valve

Insulating
Cover

T&P
Overflow
Pipe

Gas Line
with connector

18-inch
Platform

provide a good seal, gasoline vapors can build up on the floor of the garage. When they reach the pilot flame or operating burner of the water heater, ignition can take place. The result will be a devastating explosion. With eighteen inches or more clearance from the floor, it would take the vapors many hours to rise to the level of the pilot flame. If there is any cross ventilation in the garage, chances are that the vapors will be swept away before they ever reach ignition. In any case, the code gives a home-owner time to do something *before* disaster strikes.

Before a home can be sold in some jurisdictions, unenclosed gas heaters mounted directly on a garage floor must be elevated and replumbed to code.

It should be noted that solar and electric water heaters do not require the eighteen-inch platform in garages. Platforms are required only where the water is heated by burner flames.

SPECIAL NOTE: A great many jurisdictions require that special drain pans be installed beneath water heaters that are located on the second or higher floor of a residence. These pans must be equipped with a drain line that is capable of removing the discharge from a tripped temperature and pressure relief valve, or from a fast-leaking tank. The rule of thumb is that if water leaking or discharging to the floor would damage the floor or any lower levels, a special drainage pan should be installed.

Now look around the water heater. Is there debris or junk piled so as to obstruct the firebox door of gas, oil, or coal-fired heaters?

Do you see stains on the floor, in a circle around the water heater base? Do you see a great deal of dampness in that area? This could be a sign of a tank about to rupture, or one that has already developed a crack in its tank and has a slow leak.

It would be a good idea to get your GARDEN HOSE and attach it to the drain valve at the base of the water heater. After you've coupled it, turn on the valve. Go and look at the water coming out of the hose. If it is spewing black silt or comes out full of other colored particles, the tank has not been flushed out for a long time. (In a well-maintained home this should be done every six months.) If no water at all comes out, the heater has probably never been flushed since it was installed. It cannot operate economically because the mineral build-up in the bottom acts as insulation against heat rising from the burner. These conditions spell potential tank failure.

Fortunately, replacement water heaters are not too expensive. A faulty one should not prevent you from purchasing an otherwise desirable property. From the viewpoint of convenience, however, detecting a faulty water heater before you move in will give you a better perspective on the work you'll need to do.

[83] Be sure that there is a water heater water supply valve in place on the cold-water side of the heater (figure 22). Without the required valve, the heater will be difficult to replace. You won't be able to isolate the hot-water supply to the house fixtures without shutting off the main house water supply valve. If you discover that there is no main valve, your only option will be to go out to the meter to shut down the entire water supply to the property before the heater can be replaced. This plumbing defect can make the servicing of damaged or worn fixtures not served by their own individual angle stops (valves) a frustrating experience, at best.

[84] Of paramount importance is the condition of the vent that carries the waste gases off from the water heater burners. It should be *intact*. All joints of the flue pipe should be tightly attached to each other, and the whole system should be solidly supported with plumber's steel-perforated tape, made fast to solid wood. If the vent extends for some distance, additional bracket supports should be added to ensure good overall vent integrity. The vent should rise continuously from the top of the water heater to the flue exit in the ceiling, or through the wall. If the heater vents through an outside wall, be sure that the exposed flue is well attached to the house siding with proper brackets, that it extends to at least twelve inches above the roof, and that it terminates with a proper flue cap.

Examine the flue as carefully as you can. It should have *no holes* or *cracks* in it, and each section *must be securely joined* to the next.

If the heater vent joins a larger venting system, such as that coming from a furnace or boiler, be absolutely sure that it rises continuously from the water heater to the junction of the larger pipe. Flue gases will not completely exhaust from the system if the pipe goes downhill. *A badly installed vent can be life-threatening.*

(SPECIAL NOTE: Electric and solar water heaters do not require vents.)

[85] Be sure that every water heater has an automatic temperature and pressure relief valve. This important device is your only insurance against a malfunction of the water heater. It is easily identified (figure 23). A pipe should be fastened to the T&P valve. It is designed to carry away the steam when the valve opens to relieve excess pressure. This line should terminate outside of the building, at a floor drain, or should end no higher than six inches from the floor near the water heater.

[86] The furnace or space heaters are very difficult to evaluate without fuel or power. They should be examined superficially, after you've finished looking at the water heater. Central-heating plants are usually lo-

Figure 23.

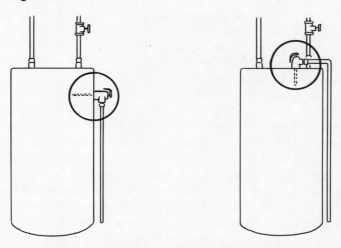

**Automatic Temperature and Pressure Relief Valve
typical configurations**

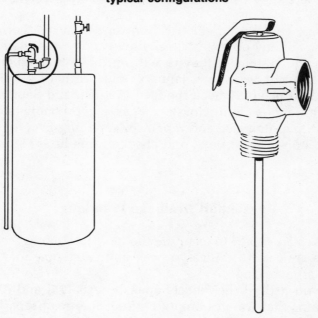

cated near the water heaters in larger homes. In smaller ones, they can be situated in special closets on the main floor of the home. Wherever located, they should be in an environment that is free of debris and materials stored so as to obstruct easy access to the burners, blowers, and controls. Wall heaters should give no signs of sooting (black shadows) on their decorative outer housings or on the walls above them.

[87] You must examine a furnace vent with the same care as you checked the water heater flue in [84] above. The same rules apply. It must be sound, solidly supported, well made, and continuously rising to its exit from the room or building. It is very difficult to check the vents on individual wall panel heaters. They rise from the top of each unit, inside the walls. The only test that has any meaning requires that the gas be on. In that procedure, you fire up the heaters and check the walls directly above the heaters in about an hour. If the walls are very hot, the heaters should be checked by a competent heating-and-ventilating specialist.

Thermostats should be located well away from heater outlets and, in hot-water- or steam-heated dwellings, should not be located over active registers or where they can be directly affected by baseboard heaters of any kind.

In many cases, you'll need electrical power to test the thermostats.

In the absence of any other tests, ask the owners what their experience has been with the system. If they're willing, have them show you their fuel bills for the prior December, January, and February. (In the southern hemisphere you'd need to check the July, August, and September bills.)

From your initial questioning of the owner, you probably have the name of the installer, maintenance and repair, or servicing firm for the heating system. If you don't, get it now, and check on the house's heating plant with them.

Waste and Drainage Plumbing

Granted, it takes an expert to examine the house's drainage system properly, but there are certain things you can do to get some idea of how the house sewers are working.

[88] When you had all the faucets open in tests [75] and [76], did you notice any drains that weren't emptying their fixtures properly? If so, go back and try them again. If the drains still run slowly, you know that the fixtures involved will require service. Either you or a serviceperson will have to clear the slow-running drains.

If all but a fixture or two drain quickly and completely, chances are that the main drainage plumbing is in reasonably good condition. If *everything* drains slowly, the system will need a thorough examination and clearance. For this you'll probably need professional help.

[89] Flush the toilets. In this test you will be checking three things:

[90] Observe how fast the water closet empties. When it vortexes to flush down material in the bowl, does it make a nice large funnel or does it make a lazy, thin funnel-like fissure down into the sump? Flush down a piece of tissue. See how it goes down. The vigor of the flushing action is an indication of the condition of both the water closet's trap system and the house's main sewer line.

[91] As the tank is refilling, lift the tank lid off and look inside as the water level climbs. Notice if water from the ballcock (float or floatless tank-filling valve) squirts upward and around the tank willy-nilly. It should be reasonably quiet. The water should discharge into the tube going into the overflow, and from the bottom of the valve only. Refilling action should be brisk, rising to full within two minutes. Failure to meet any one of these criteria is grounds for concern and could herald short-term repairs. If the float is set too high, the water level will rise higher than the overflow tube, which will keep the valve operating continuously—not a very good situation.

[92] Look down into the bottom of the tank. There should be a flush-valve. The flush-valve is rubber, usually black, but it can be red or any other color. It is normally attached to a brass rod or flapper assembly (with a chain). When the toilet flush-lever is operated, it pulls the rubber cone (or semisphere) up and out of its seat, which allows the water to discharge into the bowl. If this rubber flush-valve fails to seat properly, it allows annoyingly constant drainage into the bowl. This, in turn, causes the ball cock to discharge water into the tank at a slow dribble, creating a steady humming or high-pitched hissing sound, which most folks find very disturbing at night.

You should know that if a toilet tank lid is missing, it is nearly impossible to purchase a replacement from any but a plumbing jobber, wholesaler, or an old-time master plumber with a storage room full of old toilet parts. Special-order tank lid replacements can cost as much as the entire water closet did on the day it was bought.

Look at the toilet base. Notice if the grout (sealing mortar) is still in place. Note any odors in the room, and be careful to examine the tiles around the water closet. Wetness, cracked or missing grout around the base, and serious staining and wetness in the tile grout are definite problem signs.

It is also a good idea to test the stability of the water closet itself. Put the lid down and sit on it. Try to rock it back and forth and from front to rear. A well-installed toilet should be solid and steady in its place.

During bathroom examinations you should always look for any noticeable wetting and staining. Odors can come from sink and bathtub traps that let sewer gases escape from fixtures that haven't been used for an extended period of time. Check this by opening the water tap in a fixture for about a minute. Then turn it off and go away. Return later to see if the odors are as strong as before. Persistent sewage odors anywhere in the house are a real *danger* sign: something is wrong with the house sewer system.

[93] Turn on the dishwasher. Let it run through one complete cycle while you inspect other areas and fixtures. It doesn't matter that it's empty and there's no soap. What you're looking for is full and effective functioning, which includes filling, washing action, emptying, drying action and effective controls. Cold water is just fine for this test.

[94] Get the sink water running and test the garbage disposer. Let it run for a minimum of thirty seconds, with both hot and cold water taps wide open. Then turn off the disposer and let the water continue to run. After about fifteen seconds, turn off the water and notice how long it takes the water to drain, *without* the disposer in operation. Extremely slow drainage can indicate a blockage in the waste line. Often, it can be remedied with a household plunger. If not, a plumber will be needed.

[95] Any other built-in or free-standing fixtures or plumbing appliances that are a part of the sale should be operated and checked for effectiveness. This might include clothes washers and instantaneous hot-water heaters, if there is electric power available, plus water softeners, filters, and pressure-reducing valves. Some of these items are not easily checked during an inspection of this type. At least query the owners, or, if you can get the name of the family plumber, you can ask him about the condition and operation of the property's appliances and fixtures.

Radon Gas

[96] IMPORTANT WARNING: Since 1981, warnings have been sounding in the U.S. media about the danger—in certain regions of the country—of radon gas emissions into unprotected structures. The July 22, 1985, issue of *Time* magazine, reported on radon, "The colorless, odorless killer: A million U.S. homes may be contaminated by deadly radon."

Radon gas is a so-called noble gas that is 7-½ times as heavy as air. It is the product of uranium breaking down deep in the earth. As the ground moves and topography changes over time, small amounts of gas reach the surface and diffuse into the atmosphere. If structures are built over exhausting fissures, they are likely to be contaminated with this dangerous gas. Because it is heavier than air, the gas usually seeks the lowest level in a building where it lies and builds up until it is stirred by movement. It can then move into living areas and be breathed.

Fortunately, there is an effective test for radon emissions. It is a charcoal-based detector available from the University of Pittsburgh Department of Physics for about ten dollars.

If you are located in one of the areas known to be affected by higher than average radon gas concentrations, such as Idaho; Montana; Grand Junction and Colorado Springs, Colorado; Fargo, North Dakota; Oak Ridge and eastern Tennessee; Damascus, Missouri; the Mount Airy, Maryland area; Pittsburgh, Boyertown, Philadelphia, and eastern Pennsylvania; Princeton, New Jersey; New York; central Maine, and Florida, by all means insist on radon emissions testing of properties you are seriously considering buying. If you are in doubt about radon conditions in your region, contact your local EPA (Environmental Protection Agency) office.

A special vapor barrier and proper venting can prevent radon gas from infiltrating into residences. This method is described in detail in the November 1987 issue of *Popular Science Monthly*.)

The Electrical System

[97] The first things to look at are the lighting fixtures. Look at the mounting bases. Are they tight to the ceilings and walls? Do the fixtures themselves appear to be sturdy, well made, and solidly mounted? If they hang from chains, in most cases you can see the wires running from their bases to the light receptacles. Are the wires smooth and intact? Is there fraying or any bare copper showing? Either can be dangerous. There must not be any splices or taped-up joints in any fixture. The code requires that all fixture wires be in one piece from the socket to the ceiling or wall box.

[98] Take careful note of the wall receptacles. Current codes presuppose that no appliance cord should have to be longer than six feet, which means that wall receptacles should be no farther than twelve feet apart. In addition, the first power receptacle in a room should be within six feet of the entrance. The code also requires that there be a receptacle in all spaces more than two feet wide (e.g., between two doors hung on a short span of wall).

[99] Code requires grounded receptacles (figure 24). The three-prong

Figure 24.

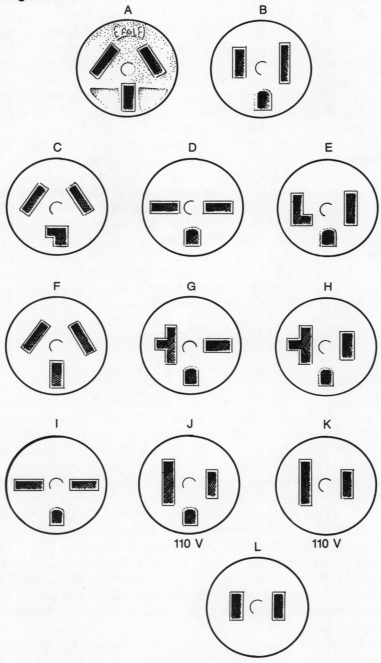

receptacle is considered the safest type (example J). If the house has only the two-bladed receptacles, they should be the polarized type (example K), with a larger negative than positive slot.

NOTE: Unless you have some experience working with electricity or wiring, have an electrician perform the following test for you.

To see whether a two-blade system is properly grounded, take your MULTITESTER, set it for continuity testing (ohms), insert one of the test leads into the negative blade slot (usually the larger of the two), and then touch any water pipe or faucet with the other lead (see figure 25A). (The bathroom or kitchen is a good place to do this.)

REPEAT WARNING: IF THE POWER IS ON, DO NOT TEST WITH THE MULTITESTER SET FOR CONTINUITY. WITH THE POWER ON, MAKE SURE TO USE THE "AC VOLTS" SETTING.

With the tester set for continuity, the needle should swing a full arc to the right on the dial. Now touch the screw that holds the receptacle plate in place with one lead, and touch a pipe or faucet with the other. Again, the needle should swing. If nothing happens with either test, there is serious doubt that the electrical system is grounded, an INCREDIBLY DANGEROUS situation. It may be necessary to check the receptacle from the smaller blade side to ground if there is no reading. Sometimes do-it-yourselfers and I-don't-give-a-damn handymen pay no attention to the blade polarity. If you get a positive reading (as above) from your meter, between the smaller blade slot and the pipe or faucet, make a note to check other receptacles in the house to ground. If some are grounded to the wide-blade side, and others to the narrow-blade side, it is possible that a nasty dead short may occur someday. This is again an incredibly dangerous situation that you will *have* to correct if you purchase the property.

IMPORTANT SPECIAL NOTE: Any electrical receptacles located in bathrooms, in kitchens within five feet of sinks, and on the outside of the house *must* be of the "ground fault interrupter" type. Some codes do not require this type of receptacle in kitchens, but they do increase safety, and are therefore recommended. In general, ground fault interrupter–type receptacles are strongly advised wherever it is possible for a person to touch water and a power receptacle at the same time.

The ground fault interrupter is easy to identify. It is usually a double receptacle with a reset button in plain view. Some have small LED glow lights that indicate when the circuit has been interrupted. Interruption occurs whenever the ground is faulted (nonoperational or severed). As soon as that happens, the power to the receptacles is cut off. The recep-

Figure 25.

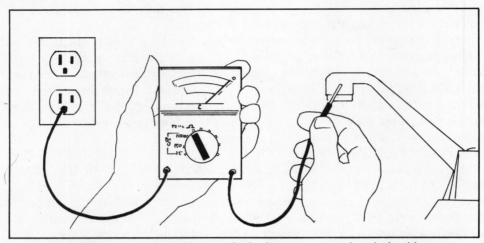

A. Defective ground showing continuity between ground and plumbing

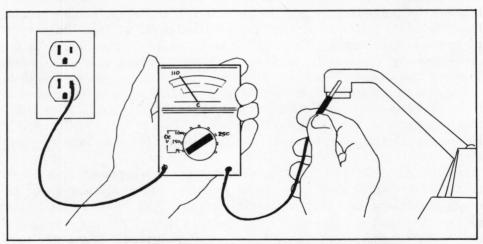

B. Power on, showing that plumbing is shorting to power plug

tacles cannot be used again until the ground is satisfactorily restored and the unit reset.

[100] When the two blade slots are of equal size (example L), make a note that you should have them changed to the three-prong type as soon as you take possession. CAUTION: Such replacement can take place only if the house system is grounded to each wall box (plate screw). *Do not*

replace two-prong receptacles with three-prong receptacles if the system is an ancient, ungrounded two-wire system. Someone could think that the new receptacles are safe and find out later, after having been shocked, that the new receptacles were merely ornamental.

Two-blade receptacles can be tested as described above, but you won't know which side is negative, so you'll have to try both blade slots, through your tester, to the ground (pipe or faucet). Again, test the plate screw to ground. If you do not get a reading, chances are that the house system is a two-wire system, without ground of any kind, or that the separate ground wire, demanded by even the most ancient electrical codes, is no longer effective.

[101] It is important to realize that if, for any reason, there is no grounding to the third or grounding prong of *three-prong* electrical receptacles, it is the same as no grounding to the screw of two-prong receptacles. *No ground is no ground,* and it's very hazardous. There is special danger in wet locations, as in the kitchen and utility areas.

The true ground on two-prong receptacles is to the plate screw. That's why when you buy adapters from three-prong plugs to two-blade plugs for insertion into two-slot receptacles, there is a small wire with a screw lug on the end of it. That lug is meant to be fastened to the screw in the plate to ground it, *if the house system is grounded.*

[102] Power-on testing: With the electrical power on, set your MULTITESTER to "AC Volts—250" or any setting above 125 volts.

Your reading will come from bridging the MULTITESTER from the positive (smaller) slot to a ground (pipe or faucet). CAUTION: DON'T ALLOW ANYONE NEAR THE GROUND WHEN YOU ARE TESTING, AND DON'T TOUCH EITHER THE METAL TEST LEAD TIPS OR THE PIPE OR FAUCET WITH YOUR FINGERS WHILE TESTING (see figure 25B).

Now, when you test, the actual current will be passing through the meter, and you will get a true voltage reading at the receptacle. The needle will normally not travel farther than one-third to two-thirds of the way across the dial, depending on the setting. You should not get a reading from the negative blade slot or the third prong of a three-prong receptacle to the pipe or faucet. If you do, the receptacle has reverse polarity and may be DANGEROUS.

SPECIAL NOTE: Recently a new device has come onto the market that automatically checks the polarity of three-prong receptacles. The one with which I've been experimenting is called the "Snapit Circuit Tester"—which I strongly recommend. It can be used only when the electricity is on. This useful product retails at about five dollars, and is well worth the investment.

[103] Interestingly enough, many beautifully maintained, expensive homes have no grounding system at all. There are many reasons for it, and they all render the house power system extremely hazardous. Since most home electrical systems are grounded to the metal pipes in the house's plumbing, the most common cause of a failed ground is the installation of plastic pipe somewhere between the water meter and the house. Plastic is an insulator, and if plastic pipe is introduced into the plumbing, the house water system will no longer be grounded to earth. To further complicate matters, in a great many areas the utilities' pipelines from water meters to mains are made of plastic or Transite. In these cases, on-site protected grounding becomes a matter of installing grounding rods.

Very few handymen, gardeners, and do-it-yourselfers realize that when they replace old, corroded galvanized-steel pipe with the new high-tech, state-of-the-art plastic water supply pipe, they are disconnecting the grounding system of the house at the same time. Experienced journeyman plumbers have been known to make the same mistake. It is always good to check.

A savvy contractor will install a code-approved grounding rod to replace a nullified ground.

Another frequent cause of failed grounds is the installation of so-called dielectric unions on water heaters, and separating copper pipe from galvanized-steel pipe elsewhere in the water supply system. (Dielectric unions reduce galvanic corrosion where metal pipes of dissimilar materials are joined.) In order to maintain a proper electrical ground whenever these insulating unions are installed, a jump wire should be installed, although that defeats the purpose of the dielectric unions. For that reason, the jump wires are seldom installed, and the house can very easily end up without its essential electrical ground.

In some districts, the utility will require that all metal piping—both water and gas (fuel)—in the structure be grounded.

IMPORTANT NOTE ON GROUNDING: The best way to check general grounding to the pipe system is to wrap and cinch a bare wire around the main house-to-meter water pipe just as it goes into the ground, and another one around a cold-water pipe coming out from the wall beneath any plumbing fixture in the house. Touch the two free ends with your MULTITESTER leads, which should be set for "continuity" (ohms). The needle should swing all the way to the right. If it doesn't, there is no ground. A positive reading on this test is final evidence of a good house common ground to the piping system. The only way this test can be defeated is if plastic pipe has been connected to the metal pipe beneath the surface of the earth. In that case, there will be some ground. To confirm the condition, ask the owners whether or not a plastic main was installed. If the answer is yes, make a note to have an electrician implant a code-approved grounding rod.

Here is how the grounding system must be installed. In a three-wire system, the white wire coming in from the utility is neutral, and it is the system ground. If for any reason that line snaps or is otherwise interrupted, there would be no neutral and no ground from the utility, and the house system would be extremely dangerous. The electrical code therefore requires a *redundant* system of grounding.

The entrance service box must be grounded to two places: through a grounding rod to earth, and to the house's metal piping. Alternately, the pipe can be grounded directly to the grounding rod. In this situation, since the entrance service is grounded to the grounding rod and the pipes are also grounded to the same rod, it has the same effect as the entrance service being grounded to the pipe through a separate line.

The pipe must be grounded to the primary ground—the grounding rod. The entrance service box must have the white wire from the utility fastened to a grounding bus-bar. That bus-bar should contain all the white (netural/negative) wires and all of the grounding (bare copper or green-jacketed) wires coming from the house system or from subfeed boxes (interior breaker boxes or panels) to breakers or fuses in the entrance service panel.

Often the house's pipe network will also be grounded to interior breaker boxes or panels at the ground bus-bar. The subfeed panel or box is grounded to the entrance service panel through the metal conduit that joins them or by a green-jacketed or bare copper ground lead attached to the *uninsulated* bus-bar. A suitably sized white wire will be attached from the entrance service to the *insulated* bus-bar in the subfeed (interior breaker box)—as are all the white wires from the various circuits.

Remember that the *uninsulated* bus-bar receives the bare copper or green-jacketed ground wires coming from the entrance service panel and from each interior house circuit. *Interior panels and boxes must not commingle bare copper (green-jacketed) grounds and white neutral wires. The only place that should happen is in the main entrance service.*

If it is impossible to achieve grounding from the house piping system for any reason, then all the interior panels and boxes must be grounded directly to the primary grounding rod, to which the entrance service is attached.

I consider the foregoing section to be the most important in this manual. Read it over several times. If you have any questions or doubts about how the electrical system should look—or how it works—leave this testing to an experienced electrician.

[104] Try the house switches. If you have the time, take a SCREW-

DRIVER from your kit, remove the switchplate, and unscrew the switch from its box. It is best to check one or two switches. It is especially useful to do this with switches that "feel wrong."

[105] WARNING: Don't attempt to examine any switches with the power on, unless you are experienced in such work.

With the power off, switches can be tested with your MULTITESTER. Simply place your test leads on the two screws to which the black and white wires are connected. (IMPORTANT: THE METER MUST BE SET TO "CONTINUITY" [OHMS]. Unscrew all the lights in the circuit.) With the switch in the closed (on) position, the needle should swing all the way to the right. In the open (off) position, the needle should not react.

There are many types of switches available today. The oldest models click audibly when you turn them off and on. Other, later versions are completely silent and do not snap into place when operated.

[106] If you do unscrew switchplates and check installations, be especially careful to note the condition of the wires. The insulation should be intact, and there should be no bare wires that can come into contact with the box itself when the switch block is returned to its original position.

With the electricity on, the whole test process is quite easy. If the lights light and the switchable wall receptacles get power when you turn on the switches, you're in business.

[107] IMPORTANT NOTE: When a switch is closed, turning ON the attached light or appliance, the handle should be in the *up* position. The *down* position is *always* OFF. The exceptions are three- and four-way switches, where lights or appliances are controlled from more than one switch.

If you see any sparking when you operate a switch, it could be defective or badly worn, but some types do spark when they're new. It's best to be safe. If the switch's appearance or operation is suspicious, make a note that it should be checked.

[108] If you notice that a light bulb flickers when it is turned on, it could be caused by a switch that has seen better days. It may also be a problem with the light socket, or the wiring between the switch and the fixture. A constantly flickering light bulb is a sign of potential danger. The exceptions are:

1. If the other lights in the *same* fixture burn steadily, the offending bulb is probably about to burn out—or the socket is defective.

2. If all the lights in the house flicker, it could be a sign of a "brownout," or power problems in the utility's grid. In that case, other houses in the area will be affected. If the house under inspection is the only residence affected, there may be defects or excessive wear in the main switch, main breakers, or in the incoming power link. Problems in this

category should be referred to the local utility company for inspection and recommendations or repair.

Check to see if an offending bulb is screwed into its socket properly, and throw the switch more than once. If you still get flickering, make a note that the circuit must be checked soon.

If you notice the lights dimming when the washer, garbage disposer, refrigerator, or other appliance is turned on, question the house power first. The temporarily lowered light level is a sign of an overloaded circuit.

[109] Wherever you can, check the house wiring. This is usually possible in cellars, basements, and attics. Old wiring ordinarily took the form of two separate wires, supported by ceramic or Bakelite insulators nailed onto studs in the walls, ceilings, and floor joists.

[110] Where this type of wiring passes through wood, it should be encased in ceramic tubes to keep the wires from rubbing on sharp wood edges. In some areas, these ceramic tubes have been replaced by treated fiber sleeves called "looms." Again, the reasons for their existence are clear. Wood expands, contracts, and moves in a structure. Heat and cold make house framing move significantly through the four seasons. Wire lengthens and thins, contracts and thickens within its insulating jacket. The jacket itself has its own rate of expansion and contraction. The fiber sleeves and ceramic tubes were designed to allow contraction and expansion within wood and metal structures without damage to wiring. If they are missing, a hazardous condition exists.

When house wiring is overloaded with appliances and lights, fuses blow. Some folks, tired of continually replacing fuses, simply upgrade the capacity. Where there was a 15-ampere fuse, they install a 20. If they still have problems, they go all the way up to a 30-ampere fuse. This can permit the wire to overheat, causing the insulation to become brittle and, in many cases, to crack and drop away in large pieces.

[111] Extensive evidence of brittle insulation is a WARNING of possibly dangerous shorts and power system breakdown within the forseeable future.

IMPORTANT WARNING: Ordinary brown, cream, or white two-conductor extension cords, commonly referred to as "zip" cord or wire, *must not be permanently stapled or otherwise attached to any surface. It must not be laid beneath carpeting.* This material is not designed for permanent installation and can deteriorate rapidly in such service, rendering it extremely dangerous. If you notice any code violations of this type, realize that they must be corrected immediately.

[112] Modern house wiring is generally of the "romex" variety. Romex is easy to identify—it is usually three wires encased in a tough rubbery

or plastic jacket. If the jacket is peeled back, normally there would be a black-insulated conductor (positive), a white-insulated conductor (negative), and a bare conductor (ground). Most often, these conductors are made of copper wire. The gauges for copper wire are normally fourteen for 15 amperes of conducted electricity, twelve for 20 amperes, and ten for 30 amperes.

The outer jackets of romex house wiring can be black, gray, or white.

[113] If the conductors (wires) are silver, they are probably aluminum. At this point, I must sound a WARNING! Aluminum wiring has had a record of failure over the years. Much aluminum house wiring was manufactured and installed during and shortly after World War II and the Korean conflict to conserve strategic copper. If this material was installed without taking proper precautions, it can cause overheating wherever it is connected to a receptacle, panel, or fixture.

As a general rule, I recommend replacement of all aluminum house wiring with copper. By house wiring I mean the small services to lights and receptacles. If complete replacement is not feasible, then the least that must be done is to be sure that every connection from aluminum wiring to any receptacle or fixture be made to contacts especially designed for aluminum wire. Quite a few homes have been retrofitted with these special receptacles and fixture mountings, which is much less expensive than rewiring an entire house. Retrofitting of this type is *not* a suitable do-it-yourself project. Licensed professional electricians must be hired.

[114] Main cables from weatherheads or from the utility's grid have usually been installed by professionals who knew what they were doing. Aluminum cables installed from entrance services to subpanels (interior breakers) should be carefully examined periodically for overheating. A professional, licensed master electrician (electrical contractor) should be called in to do this examination. If necessary, he should refasten each cable to its terminal, using the graphitic bonding compounds designed to prevent the problems I've described above.

CAUTION: Romex wiring can become brittle from overheating, exactly the same as the older wiring. Overheating usually results from loose connections and/or significant overload. Look for discoloration and glazing or brittleness on romex jackets. Extensive damage to wiring usually requires costly replacement of runs or entire systems.

[115] If you have the time, check the subpanel wiring for proper sizing. If you take the breaker panel face off, you will be able to see the wires coming into each breaker or fuse. Modern romex is marked with the wire size. Fourteen-gauge wire usually is imprinted "14–2," which means

fourteen-U.S.-gauge two-conductor wire, with a ground (third uninsulated wire). Twelve-gauge is called 12–2, and ten-gauge is 10–2.

A 15-ampere breaker or fuse should not have any wire lighter than 14–2 romex or a fourteen-gauge single *black* wire attached to it. This refers to copper wire only. Aluminum wire must be one size larger. In this case it must be 12–2 aluminum wire romex for a 15-ampere breaker or fuse.

A 20-ampere breaker or fuse needs 12–2 (twelve-gauge) copper wire or 10–2 aluminum wire romex.

A 30-ampere breaker or fuse needs 10–2 (ten-gauge) copper wire or 8–2 aluminum wire romex.

(I'm sure you've noticed that wire becomes heavier as the gauge number gets smaller.)

[116] It is also important to know that ONLY black and red wires should be attached to breakers or fuses. The white wires should be common to each other, and attached to the same bus-bar. As mentioned before, except in the entrance service, the bare ground wires should be attached to a separate bus-bar, and MUST be in common as well. Quite often you find both the white conductors and the ground wires attached to the same bus-bar. Even though this practice is prohibited in the new codes, there isn't much you can do about it without professional assistance. It IS important, however, that black be positive, and that the routine of black to black, white to white, and ground to ground be observed throughout the entire electrical system of any house.

CAUTION: There is an exception to the like-color–to–like-color rule. The meaning of the color of a wire jacket can be changed simply by attaching a piece of colored electrician's tape to the wire. A black wire with a piece of white tape around it can be considered to be a white lead. A white wire with black tape is positive as surely as if it had black insulation. Green is the color of an insulated ground wire. Green tape over any other color is an indication of ground. A red wire is ordinarily the second ''hot'' wire in a 220–240–volt circuit, so all red wires should be handled as if they were black (positive) leads. Always be careful of black and red wires, wherever you see them, unless they have the identifying tape changes mentioned above.

[117] If the house is wired for an electric stove, it should have the correct power receptacle in place. See figure 24 (example A). Please take note: The receptacle may be installed either as shown or upside down.

[118] If the house is wired for an electric clothes dryer, it should have the receptacle shown in figure 24 (example C). Again, it may be installed as shown or upside down.

[119] While you're about it, take a good look at the air discharge vent

for the clothes dryer. It should be located a foot or so from the floor, in the vicinity of the power receptacle. It should go through an outside wall and have a flapper vent valve on the outside to keep rain and wind from getting into the pipe. This vent and flap are usually manufactured as a unit. The pipe is most often three or four inches in diameter and made from galvanized, tin- or cadmium-plated steel. Recently, many models have been manufactured from aluminum or plastic.

[120] A gas clothes dryer must have a proper natural gas or LPG (liquid petroleum gas) supply line, complete with a gas cock or valve. If there is nothing but a capped pipe end to which the connection must be made, realize that the main gas valve must be turned off for repairs or replacement, or when the dryer is moved. The code requires a gas cock. The line should be a minimum of half-inch black or galvanized steel. Now and then you'll find that the gas line terminates with a gas cock and a special corrugated or smooth copper connector tube. That's okay. It will make your hookup that much easier.

[121] It should be noted that gas dryers exhaust the products of combustion through the hot-air vent described in [119] above.

[122] Many codes require a range hood over the kitchen stove (or kitchen range out West). This should be equipped with an exhaust fan or blower, which you should test for efficiency. Many of these hoods have grease collectors which resemble a frame full of bright coarse steel wool. Check the collector before you test the fan. If it is full of grease, you will not feel the air draw through the collector. A good test is to place a piece of paper against the intake. If the fan sucks enough to hold it in place, it's okay. Note that a degreasing job is an important priority. A severely stopped-up grease collector is a fire hazard. If there is no power for the fan tests, ask about its condition.

[123] Be absolutely sure that the bathroom exhaust fans are in good operating condition. Again, if there is no electricity, you'll be forced to make inquiries. Incidentally, current codes *require* these exhaust fans in all *windowless* bathrooms.

Gas Or Fuel Piping

[124] Most people neglect the inspection of obvious gas or fuel plumbing. By obvious I mean those pipes that are clearly visible. Quite often you will see them in open spaces like the garage, basement, or cellar. Wherever you see piping that is not a part of the house water system, you can reasonably assume that it is a gas or oil line. It should be well sup-

ported, without noticeable bananas (droops) or kinks. It should terminate at appliances or fixtures with a gas cock, and either be capped or plugged. It may terminate with a combination gas cock and corrugated or smooth copper connector tube. Oil supply lines should also be valved at each appliance.

[125] The code is quite clear on the approved connector for natural gas. It should be made of corrugated metal hose, covered with a tough, resilient, protective plastic seal-coating. Bare copper can develop pinholes and kink-cracks, which may result in gas leaks. The coated variety affords an additional safety barrier. Be sure that the connector has a band with the seal of the AGA (American Gas Association) or UPC (IAPMO), indicating that it meets the standards of the Uniform Plumbing Code (International Association of Plumbing and Mechanical Officials). It is strongly recommended that each time an appliance is replaced, the connector be replaced as well, as a simple safety precaution.

[126] Be especially careful of all connections to appliances that will remain in the house as a part of the sale. If you smell gas or fuel oil around heaters and furnaces, ask questions immediately. If you notice gas or fuel odors anywhere, ask about them. Gas and fuel leaks are among the most dangerous of household hazards.

[127] The easiest and safest way to check for gas leaks is with soap or detergent and water, mixed thoroughly in an ordinary spray bottle. The proportions should be one-third detergent and two-thirds water. Spray a generous amount over the pipe joints and connectors in the suspect area. In a few seconds bubbles will begin to appear in clusters. That's a gas leak.

HINT: You can make it easier to inspect behind pipes and in other difficult-to-inspect or relatively inaccessible places by adding a mirror to your tool kit. I strongly recommend the automotive type consisting of a small mirror mounted on a swivel and long handle. Dental mirrors are also handy, but are usually more expensive and less versatile than the automotive type.

CAUTION: NEVER USE AN OPEN FLAME TO CHECK FOR GAS OR FUEL LEAKS. THE RESULTS CAN RANGE FROM SINGED EYEBROWS TO THIRD-DEGREE BURNS OR DEATH, PLUS A DEMOLISHED HOUSE.

Interior Structural Details

[128] Your eyes are the best judges of whether or not the walls and floors are plumb and square. If you have the feeling that a wall is not

plumb (exactly perpendicular to the floor) or square to its adjacent wall or the ceiling, get out your TRY-SQUARE and TORPEDO LEVEL. Your eyes have detected something, but the variance may be so slight that you don't trust your own perception. Ninety-nine percent of the time your eyes will have noticed a true misalignment. Almost always the tools will prove you right (figure 26).

Figure 26.

Checking Square, Level, and Plumb

Place the level on the floor in several places. The bubble should come to rest precisely between the two lines on the glass tube. Even the slightest out-of-center position indicates a floor out of level. Place the level on the wall vertically and look at the horizontal bubble tube. It should also rest exactly between the two scribed lines. Realize that the short TORPEDO LEVEL will only show unevenness on the surfaces it occupies. To get a more accurate picture while checking floors, place a *true* four-foot-long two- by four-inch piece of pine or fir on edge, and set your TORPEDO LEVEL on the center of the top edge. Now you are reading the level over a four-foot span of floor.

Place your square in the corners, where the walls meet. You will immediately see if they are square to each other. Do the same from the tops of the walls to the ceiling.

A house that is seriously out of plumb and square can be very difficult to work with, especially if you intend to install new cabinets, or decorate extensively.

[129] Often you'll find that out-of-square houses have out-of-square door frames, resulting in sticky doors, and unsightly door fit in frames that have tapering gaps between their casings and closed doors.

A house's quality is directly related to the care with which it has been built. A skillful, reputable builder will not put together a house that is not plumb and square *everywhere!*

SPECIAL NOTE: There have been instances where a well-built house develops sticky doors and stress cracks at the door frames. These conditions can occur after construction if the house has been built on poorly compacted fill, or over a subterranean stream of some sort. In most cases, the builder is responsible only for the actual construction of the building. Then again, there could have been earth tremors and movement in the area over a period of years.

Many conscientiously built homes have come to grief by being within critical distances of earth fault lines or superhighways. When an eighteen-wheeler goes by at seventy miles per hour, "there's a whole lot of shakin' goin' on."

Heavy vehicular traffic in any adjacent area can be a cause for concern.

[130] Flooding over the years can also result in settling foundations. There are lots of indicators for this problem. Glazed, cracked puddles of dried mud in the general vicinity are sure signs. Persistent musty and damp odors throughout the house are others. Faint water lines (high-water marks) on the siding, and brand-new construction and plastering near the foundations, are suspicious. The best test is to inspect the under-house area. If there is a crawl space beneath the house, by all means have

it inspected by a professional. The uninitiated usually are too busy dodging cobwebs and trying to avoid mud puddles and other obstacles to do a good job of crawl space inspection. Of course, if you are insistent, some of the things to look out for are leaking pipes, cracked foundations, termite hills, hanging or drooping pipes (bananas), defective pilings, piers and supports. If the house has a fireplace on the first floor, the portion of the support structure in the crawl space should be carefully examined.

Of course, the very best way to find out about local conditions is to ask a neighbor, if you're suspicious.

As a point of information, there are federal and state maps available that delineate flood zones, low-lying areas, and the locations of dams and levees.

[131] Remember those squeaky floors I told you to notice on your first walk through? Go back to them and test them again.

This time sort of bounce up and down on them. A lot of give in the center of a floor is cause for concern. A great deal of give near the walls can be dangerous. It is a possible indication that a weight-bearing wall has been removed beneath the floor without proper structural compensation, a typical do-it-yourself aberration. Unlicensed, unskilled "wood butchers" have also been known to create such hazards without realizing it. They just simply don't know the basics of structural support.

[132] In order to determine whether there is a serious problem, you must inspect the area beneath the room you are examining. If you find that a supporting wall is missing beneath the room with the springy floor, ask the owners how the floor above is supported. Hopefully, compensating structural beams were installed. If they say the house has always been that way, check with the local building department and find out if there has been an alteration permit taken for the removal of a wall. If there is no such record, have an engineer or contractor inspect the supports and give you a structural report. The sellers should be as anxious as you are to know the truth—and should bear the cost of the inspection, since they run the risk of a later lawsuit over the nondisclosure of a "red flag" defect.

[133] To determine general building quality, take your stud finder and check a few walls, moving from the left corner to the right (figure 27). There should be a vertical stud every sixteen inches. Some older homes have them in ranges from twelve inches (overbuilt) to twenty-four inches (severely underbuilt). The maximum acceptable spacing is eighteen inches. Remember, however, that the code distance is sixteen inches or less. You can do the same check on the floor joists—the same spacings apply.

Figure 27.

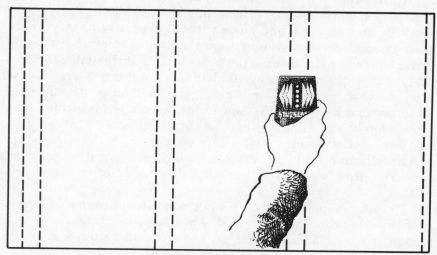

Typical Electronic Stud Finder

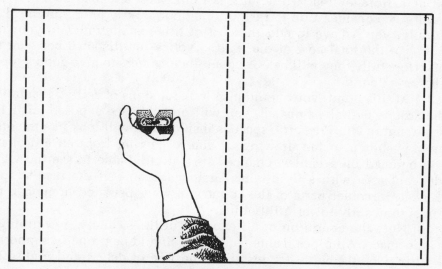

Typical Mechanical Stud Finder

[134] To determine general building maintenance, look closely at the windows and window casings. Have they been painted solidly shut over the years, or do they open and close without excessive effort? Where the windows operate on sash weights, are the cords intact and working? Is the glass clean and paint-free? Is the putty intact? Do the latches still work smoothly and well? Are all movable windows properly screened? Where metal windows open by cranking action, are the cranks still effective? Do the windows crank open easily and to the wide-open position? Do they close completely and latch without too much difficulty? Although most buyers, sellers, and agents aren't aware of it, many professional appraisers rely heavily upon this one item as an indication of the current maintenance condition of a structure. Use this information to your own advantage.

[135] The attic inspection is most important. If you cannot look into the attic because there is no ladder available, make a note to check out the space later. Of course, if there is a stairway to the attic, you will have ample opportunity now.

[136] One main consideration is whether the attic has been or can be used as a storage area. If the attic is unfinished and has no floor, you should give consideration to installing a floor shortly after you move in. Naturally, you'll have to add the cost of this installation into your calculation of the final cost of the house. Notice the distance between the joists. Hopefully they will be on sixteen-inch centers to give good support to the new floor.

[137] At this point, you should also look for signs of ceiling insulation. If the attic is partially finished, you will probably see exposed joists like those in figure 28. If the attic space is insulated, it will look like the other examples shown in the drawing. If you're peering from an attic hatch while perched on a ladder, chances are you'll be able to see the whole under-roof area with a flashlight. Again, take note of the insulation or lack of it. In cooler parts of the country, a well-insulated home can pay off in significantly lower utility bills.

[138] Note the condition of all exposed utilities, ducts, and piping in the attic space. All pipes, vents, and ducts should be properly supported. All wiring should be neatly installed and free of debris and junk. Code requires a one-inch clearance between insulation and light fixtures. Today, electric fixtures are available that are rated "insulation safe." Hot-water and solar lines should be insulated.

[139] Fireplaces and chimneys have a tendency to deteriorate rapidly. Brick chimneys are the worst of the lot from that standpoint. If you see staining where a chimney or fireplace structure goes through the ceiling, you should inspect further. Chances are that there is leaking from the

Figure 28.

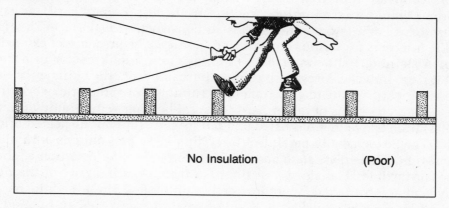

No Insulation   (Poor)

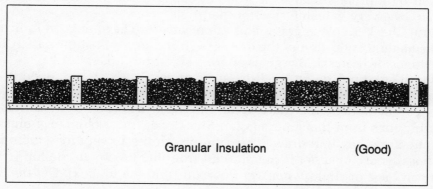

Granular Insulation   (Good)

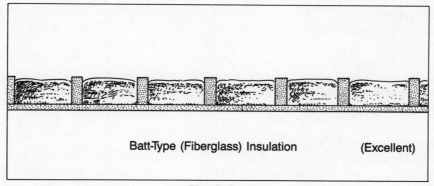

Batt-Type (Fiberglass) Insulation   (Excellent)

The Attic

roof. No matter how well insulated they are, chimneys and gas vents get warmer than the surrounding structure in the wintertime. Heat and cold cause expansion and contraction in all construction materials. This fact of life is a basis for serious concern and inquiry. The presence of extensive brown staining, with water lines running from a dark center to a light outer ring, indicates progressive water intrusion from the chimney or fireplace outward. White to gray lime lines running down the brickwork from top to base are signs of rather hard, mineral-bearing water (puddled rainwater) from above that has dried and left its signature on the heated brick.

NOTE: Be especially careful of brick fireplaces and chimneys in older homes. In some areas, state and local codes require the insertion of sheet steel or flexible steel sleeves or liners to insure the integrity of the flueway and unobstructed operation of the chimney. These should be installed by a professional. It is a rather costly process, but in the end, it preserves a very valuable asset of the property.

[140] Check fireplace grates and ash receivers. They are good indicators of the general condition of the fireplace structure. Look at the base. Check the stones or firebrick. Large gaps are a sign of trouble ahead.

[141] Look up through the fireplace damper. If it's closed, open it. If it won't open, ask the owners if the fireplace is operational, and if not, why not. You can check the draft in any fireplace with one of those instant-lighting logs from the supermarket. Remember, most chimneys must get warm before they will draw. This caution applies to very long chimneys, or those whose channel is not straight from the firebox to the top (where you can't see daylight when you look up from the firebox). *Get the owner's permission before you light any fire in the fireplace.*

SAFETY PRECAUTION: If you intend to use the fireplace in a house, a spark screen and chimney cap should be installed, if they are not already present.

[142] Ceiling stains are indications of water and soot problems. Occasionally you may see a long-running stain going from a point on the ceiling to a light fixture. The explanation for this one is simple. Moisture from above collected in the ceiling and ran toward the only place it could exit—the fixture.

Stain colors tell their own stories:

[143] Light tan or brown—Rain, tub, or shower water running between lath and plaster or through insulation onto Sheetrock. Lath and plaster stains often run in strips about a quarter-inch wide, and about one and one-half to two inches apart. Water leaking directly onto Sheetrock will accumulate and run between studs, but the stain patterns will be random.

Eventually, the water will crack the plaster or sealing surface and run out. The lighter the stain, the smaller the problem. Repetitive wettings deepen the stain, especially near the source of the leakage. If there is a bathroom or toilet room above, check for leaks from the tub through its fittings or edges (worn or fractured caulking), and through poorly maintained tile flooring. The tile caulking must be in good condition, especially where it seals against the tub apron and toilet base. Wall tile can also leak, and should be checked for watertightness. Finally, there could be a leak in the pipe connecting the valves and the shower head (figure 29). If there was a leak in the supply pipes to the valves, the ceiling would be wet all the time.

[144] Skylights are the sources of some of the more difficult leaks to remedy. What makes them such a problem is the fact that often the leak doesn't appear to be coming from the skylight frame. Sometimes it leaks into the rafters, down studs, and onto joists, and the water emerges quite a distance from the actual glazed area. Check the frame for staining and the glazing (glass or Plexiglas) for cracks and breaches in the frame.

[145] Linoleum and plastic flooring squares should be checked for seal as well. Be sure that the caulking between any flooring and the tub apron or toilet base is intact.

If there is no bathroom above the leak stains, check the roof for watertightness.

[146] Dark brown—If the stain is concentrated in one place, and is uniform in color, you're looking at a long-standing problem—which is usually caused by a roof breach. These kinds of stains are often painted over, but because paint doesn't take well on wet surfaces, you can usually find them anyway. Wherever you see "rosette" cracking (figure 30) you should suspect a "cover-up." Dark brown stains are signs of major problems and are nearly impossible to conceal.

[147] Red or reddish—Red almost always means iron or steel, although it can indicate brick in some circumstances. Poorly fired brick has been known to bleed a reddish color when water runs over it.

Ninety-nine percent of the time, red-stained ceilings indicate plumbing leaks from galvanized-steel or cast-iron soil (drainage) pipe. A small, intensely red spot is usually the sign of a galvanized-steel coupling or fitting leaking at a screw joint.

The other one percent of the time the problem is brick or sheet metal in contact with water over a period of time. It may be a sign of a roof leak. Sometimes it indicates leakage from a shower, bathroom, or toilet room that runs over other steel or iron pipes on its way to the ceiling below. Those leaks can run through the floors, down walls, or directly

Figure 29.

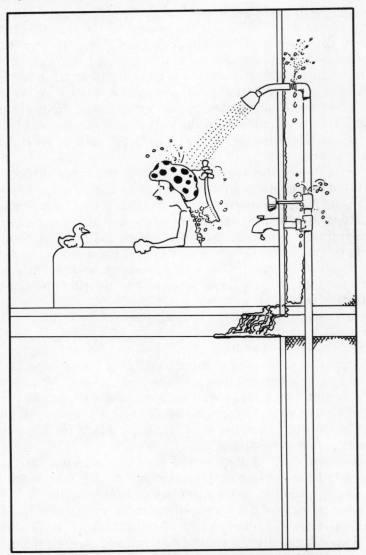

**Typical leaks in the pipe connecting the valves and
shower head, causing stains on ceiling below**

Figure 30.

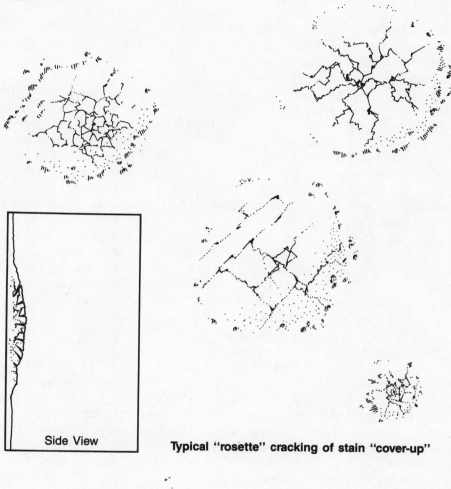

Side View

Typical "rosette" cracking of stain "cover-up"

from supply pipes leading to shower, tub, or lavatory (hand basin) faucets.

Here's one from left field: Red-stained ceilings have also resulted from water running down Sheetrock ceilings, between joists, and collecting around steel or iron light fixtures.

Red stains almost always come from rust.

[148] Black or dirty gray—Quite often sewer lines bleed a kind of black sediment with enough water to cause staining. Most of the time, though, profound black staining is a sure indicator of water running through filthy insulation or trash in attics. In very old insulated houses, where the insulation has been in place for a great many years, dust, dirt, debris, rodent droppings, and other material capable of being dissolved in water seep through to the ceiling and cause general gray staining. Quite often, these types of stains are painted out, but they will eventually reappear until the cause is eliminated.

[149] I'm sure that most of you have been in old houses where the ceilings looked as if the lathing was just about to come through the plaster. You can see every lath board clearly delineated—the ceiling has grayish, evenly spaced ridges and markings. Even when such a ceiling is repainted, it shows the telltale board marks. Such a ceiling must be Sheetrocked over the lath and plaster to look good again. There is no other remedy. If you're thinking of buying a house with this condition, the cost of this cosmetic work must be taken into account.

Another explanation of this graying phenomenon is that it can be caused by a kind of electrostatic (magnetic) action where dust and particulate matter is pulled out of the room air and sticks to the ceiling. A possible prevention is proper attic insulation above the affected area.

[150] Another cause of gray marking is soot from coal- or wood-burning stoves. Smoke tends to gather at ridges, and lath that has begun to "drop" can create the ridges. Profound gray deposits in any room with a fireplace are cause for speculation. They can indicate soot deposits from a poorly drawing fireplace or stove.

[151] Not that wood and coal stoves are the only offenders. Gravity and circulating-hot-air gas and oil furnaces discharge sooty residues and unburned products of combustion through registers into all areas of a house. This can indicate a perforated firebox or plenum, poor draft control, a plugged vent, a missing air filter, or, in the case of gas and oil furnaces, bad burner adjustment.

[152] Wherever you see wall or ceiling patches that do not conform to the surfaces around them, ask questions. The most common reasons for such patches are stains from seeping water or repairs to a hole made by

someone stepping through the ceiling while working in a crawl space or attic. A fist hole in the wall needs patching as well. These patching clues should provoke questions and require answers.

[153] Wherever green is seen, it is almost always the sign of vegetation. In a pool it is algae. It can also indicate algae growth from a long-standing leak in the ceiling. If it is bright green, the leak is still discharging sufficient oxygen-bearing liquid (fresh water) to sustain vegetable life. When the water source dries up, the algae dies and turns brown, showing the sort of lacy tracing of decayed moss. Watch out for this sign. It can mean a leak that has rusted shut, and is almost always the indication of an unsafe water system.

[154] Blue and yellow stains are the fingerprints of a bad roof. The other possibility is that someone has spilled latex paint in the rafters above. Don't laugh. It happens.

[155] Ceiling and baseboard moldings also tell interesting tales. The surest way to discover renovations or add-ons is to look at the molding strips around the edges of the ceiling and where the floor meets the wall. Generally, modern homes have no ceiling moldings unless they are replicas of older-style architecture. Baseboards are another matter. Nearly all residences have them. It's a good idea to keep an eye peeled for changes in baseboard style. The older moldings are so expensive to reproduce today that most contractors install plain, flat, no-frills strips. Run-of-the-mill do-it-yourself stores don't even stock distinctive decorative moldings of any kind.

Because of this situation, most add-ons and renovations use the plainer, less expensive materials. If you see ornate ceiling and baseboard moldings suddenly change to no ceiling moldings and plain baseboards, you can be reasonably sure that you're looking at new construction. Ask questions, and check the workmanship for flaws. A house built in a solid middle-class neighborhood before 1939 more often than not was built by a craftsman-contractor. Everything probably fit as it was supposed to, or the house wouldn't have been bought by its first owners. A modern add-on or renovation, though built of good materials by a conscientious builder or owner, will probably not fit like the original construction. It may not be as square, plumb, and true. Today's builders can't afford to be as fussy as the old-timers were, and do-it-yourselfers, in the main, lack the experience.

[156] By this time, you have seen and examined most of the points needed to form an opinion of the house's interior merits and deficiencies.

A final walk-through to verify observations is in order. Check your notes against your memory.

Summary of Critical Indicators: Inside

● Check the interior doors and windows. Doors that fit well, with properly functioning hardware, are premier signs of good craftsmanship and care.

● Make close inspections of the windows. Open and close them. If they work well, they've been well installed and well maintained.

● Note the stability of the interior floors. They should be solid underfoot, without excessive springiness.

● All surfaces should be square and plumb. A home with plumb walls, square to floors, ceilings, and corners, is getting to be more and more the exception these days.

● Pay attention to the general interior appearance. A carefully applied, attractive paint job and clean, paint-free, well-maintained hardwood floors help a lot. Wall-to-wall carpeting can hide some rather poorly finished floors beneath. Check under a rug corner and see what you can see.

● Check the plumbing and electrical installations with care. If everything is satisfactory in these departments, you've found a home that's been well maintained—and which will save you money in repairs and maintenance. Entrance electrical power service must be at least 100 amperes at 220–240 volts.

Now it's time to go outside again.

6

A Final Exterior Evaluation

You have already gathered a substantial amount of important information about the outside of the house in Chapter 3.

It may be a good idea to go back to that list to refresh your memory about any problem areas you identified on your first exterior survey, especially as they relate to roof surfaces, gutters, and concrete work.

Our final evaluation will focus almost exclusively on these problems.

Notice that all three of the items we'll examine are closely tied together . . . by *water!*

Rain, sleet, and snow falling on roofs, running off into the gutter system, eventually find their ways to the earth, either directly or over concrete surfaces. That process is one of the most erosive chains in nature. Man's puny attempts to minimize its deteriorating effects upon his machines and structures must always end in a "compromise" predicated on nature's immutable laws.

The Roof

[157] Some surfaces of a pitched roof can be seen from the ground, but for a truly thorough evaluation, someone should get up on a ladder and examine the roof carefully. An old roof looks like an old roof, from nearly every vantage. You should already have determined whether or not there are irregularities.

[158] Be especially watchful for the pitched, shingled roof that has more than three layers of composition shingles laid over a wooden-shingle base. Mixing layers of wood and composition shingles is a very poor roofing practice. In any case, the layers are usually easy to see from the ground.

Figure 31.

Water-testing the roof, gutter system, and patio patch

Too many layers puts too much weight on the roof support structure. In snow country that can lead to collapse under certain conditions.

[159] Now let's see if the roof sheds water in proper patterns without leaking. The simple answer is to flood it with water from a garden hose, and see how the runoff disposes itself to the gutter system (figure 31). Take careful note if water runs over the gutters and down the house siding—this indicates something is seriously wrong with the gutter system.

[160] There is a question whether or not the tenants or owner of a res-

96

idence will permit water testing of the roof area and gutter system. If it isn't permitted, the only thing you can do is ask the owner direct questions. Record the questions and their answers. Have them initial and date your record of the conversation if you can.

[161] An example of a poorly flashed rainwater gutter is shown in figure 32. This problem can result in serious rotting beneath the siding and in

Figure 32.

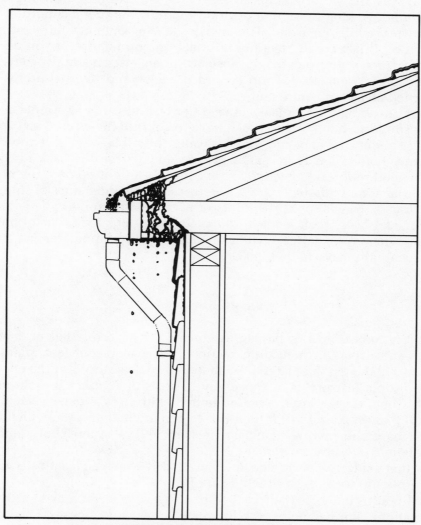

Poorly flashed rainwater gutter

the framing, and the eventual deterioration of wood siding of all types. The situation can be aggravated by heavy deposits of leaves and conifer needles (also see figure 11).

[162] Water-testing methods are shown in figures 31 and 33. Those same illustrations show the most significant water disposal patterns. These tests can answer your roof questions about whether the roof you're inspecting can dispose water runoff properly into the drainage system.

[163] It is almost impossible to assess the condition of a flat roof from the ground. Asking those in a position to know the roof's condition will yield worthwhile answers. The owner or the roofing contractor who worked on it last could have the information you require. If you can get onto the roof with your magic hose, you can test and draw your own conclusions. Water should run toward the edge and internal drains and be carried away efficiently and rapidly (figure 33).

[164] Checking for roof leaks after water testing is not as simple as you might suppose. In any case, you'll have to get into the attic, crawl space, or other under-roof area and look for water. It will be a relief if you don't find any. Before you leave—after patting yourself on the back for being such a good roof leak detective—shine your flashlight up onto the under-roof surfaces and rafters. If you see wetness on the undersides of shingles, on stringers, beams, or at the joints of plywood sheathing, you could be looking at a leaky roof. If the attic has flooring, look for traces of puddle stains. Where you notice matted or damaged insulation, realize that it will eventually have to be replaced.

Paved Surfaces

Normally, one thinks of paving as concrete. I have referred to concrete patios and drives in preceding sections. As a matter of fact, plant-mix (asphalt) is the paving material of choice in some sections of the country. Some people just prefer it, especially in areas of significant earth movement, where repairs are needed more frequently. It's a lot easier to pat in a bit of plant-mix and roll it than it is to patch with concrete, which takes a lot longer and involves much more work. What's more, hot plant-mix usually makes a neater patch.

All that aside: When I refer to concrete driveways and patios, you can substitute the word *asphalt* where applicable.

[165] Patios and slabs adjacent to buildings must pitch away from the foundations. For examples, see figures 31 and 33. In figure 31 the water runs away from the leader (downspout) and discharges to the edge of the

Figure 33.

Testing for proper disposal of water from a flat roof

patio. It also runs toward the foundation to the right of the otherwise occupied gentleman with the magazine. Water at the foundation has the potential of undermining it in time. In figure 33 the water is running away from the foundations and does not appear to be any danger to the building.

[166] If you are unable to use water, another way to test the slab pitch

Figure 34.

Testing slab pitch with rubber ball

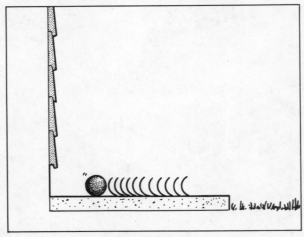

Unsatisfactory

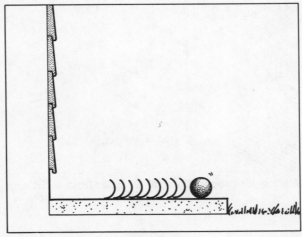

Satisfactory

is with your RUBBER BALL. The method is simple. Drop the ball straight down from an inch or two above the slab and watch which way it rolls—toward or away from the house foundations (figure 34).

[167] As a general rule, all slabs and driveways should drain to their outside edges and away from all foundations or other structures. Substantial puddling and poor drainage patterns can mean that the property needs an expensive reorientation of all offending surfaces. In layman's language that means that someone is going to have to break up the concrete, haul it out, and re-lay new concrete properly.

Poor Planning and Construction

Earlier I mentioned sewage problems due to stopped-up mains. The same problems can be caused by poorly laid or planned concrete drives.

[168] A great many crushed sewer pipes can be traced to unreinforced driveways of less than code thickness, laid over vitreous-clay, laminated-bituminous, or even service-weight cast-iron soil pipe. In the illustration (figure 35) you can see why the pipe has been crushed. First, it's too close to the slab (shallow bury). Second, it's in ground that has not been compacted to its original density. Third, the concrete slab has cracked severely and has begun to sink into the soft earth. Cracking will occur on the shear points where the undisturbed earth meets the fill. When you see these kinds of shearing cracks, *beware!* Be especially cautious when those kinds of cracks are within one to two feet of each other and parallel. That could be an indication of a buried line in soft earth.

[169] The combination of tree roots and a cracked sewer pipe can lead to an even greater problem. Raw sewage is a kind of noxious plant food. The combination of water and "fertilizer" will draw roots from great distances. They then infiltrate the pipe and fill it with roots. In this process, the roots may undermine structure foundations, walkways, and patios, and start heaving the slabs like they were so many chuck wagon pancakes. When you see heaving concrete, look for big trees nearby. Eventually, the trees will have to come out. If there is an affected sewer in the vicinity, it will have to be replaced (figure 36).

[170] While I'm talking about drainage and sewers, one of the most serious sewer problems imaginable can occur if the house sewer system is combined with the storm drains. The problem (see figure 37) is pretty much self-explanatory. Almost everywhere, the combination of storm runoff with the house sanitary system is forbidden by law. Yet it is a favorite do-it-yourself pastime, undertaken in the name of "neatness, or-

Figure 35.

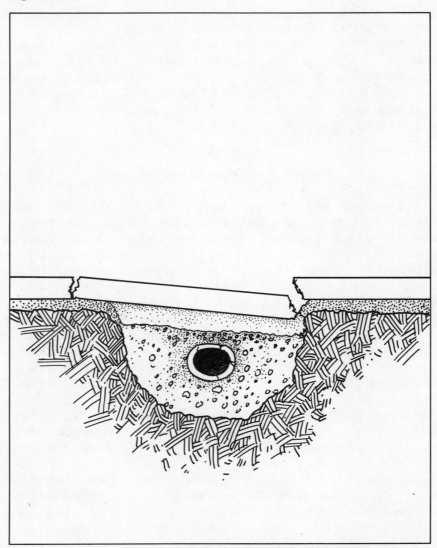

Crushed sewer pipe due to poorly planned and laid driveway

derliness, and sanitation.'' If everyone did this, the city sewer system would be overloaded in the wintertime. If your area has no separate storm drainage system, find out what the law is on combining the two systems. In most cases the city engineers will ask you to drain your storm water to the gutters. Some towns have the facilities to handle both sanitary and storm effluents in one system. They are, however, few and far between. Find out what the law says; then check the system as presently installed on the property. Where you find leaders (downspouts) from roof gutters

Figure 36.

Tree roots infiltrating a cracked sewer pipe

Figure 37.

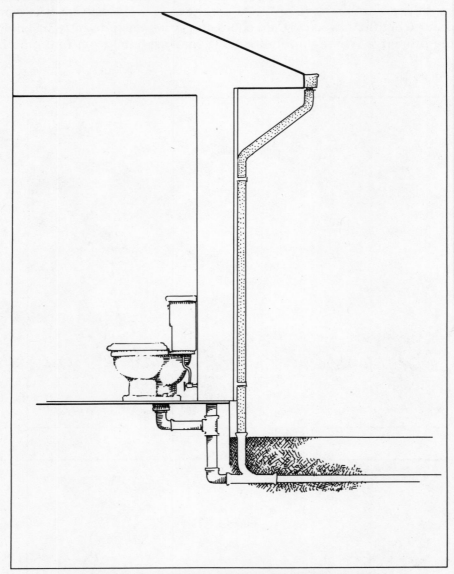

**Storm drain combined with house sanitary system
(ILLEGAL almost everywhere)**

draining to neat hubs near the foundations, ask the owner where the water goes. If it goes into the sanitary sewer system, and the city says it shouldn't, somebody's going to have to spend some money to make the system legal.

Summary of Critical Indicators: Outside

- Look at the overall neatness and appearance of the lawns and gardens. Well-manicured surroundings are a positive point—they indicate that the property has been well maintained.
- Check the general appearance of the building, including its roof, porches, decks, and siding. A well-maintained older home can be a good buy. A neglected newer house can end up being a dog that is expensive to repair and maintain.
- Note the appearance and fit of the doors and windows. Well-painted and maintained sashes, and doors that work smoothly and well are hallmarks of conscientious builders and owners.
- Be sure to check for, the presence or absence of a house main water valve. Without that valve, plumbing repairs and maintenance can be chores. In an older home, it shows a lack of concern and knowledge that can be reflected elsewhere in more critical areas.
- Finally, note the appearance of the outside gutter system and concrete surfaces. Poor showings in either of these critical items can be indications of general deterioration throughout the property. Well-maintained gutters, sidewalks, and patios are very positive indicators.

Evaluating Special Installations

The Swimming Pool

There isn't another facility on a residential property that's more difficult to maintain than a swimming pool. There's no question that a poorly maintained pool can be the bane of happy family life. It is also true to say that there is no recreational facility more enjoyable than a well-kept swimming pool.

Your job will be to check the pool out and form a good impression of its condition—whether it needs repairs, and how difficult or expensive it will be to maintain. If you're not familiar with the technical aspects of residential swimming pools, what I'm about to advise can seem like a terrible chore. Perhaps you should consider checking with the pool maintenance company in the neighborhood. The seller should bear the cost of having someone from the company come out and do a complete survey. Easier still, get the name of the firm that has been working on the pool from the owner, and give them a call.

As an aside, it might be better to get an unbiased opinion from a disinterested expert. By the time you've gotten down to inspecting the pool, you are probably sold on the other aspects of the property, but a pool complex that needs mechanical and structural rehabilitation can constitute an incredible expense item.

POINT OF INFORMATION: The current National Electrical Code has set new, very strict electrical grounding regulations for swimming pools, spas, and hot tubs, contained within Section 680 of the code. Almost none of the existing swimming pools, spas, and hot tubs conform to the new code; they will probably be considered to be "grandfathered," and will not be required to be modified to conform. In some strict-observance areas of the country, however, full conformance could be required as a precondition for the resale of a property with an out-of-code swimming pool, spa, or hot tub. For this reason, you should be aware of the code changes and your local standards. If conformance is required, all modifications must be made by a licensed master electrician (electrical contractor). This is a significant red-flag item.

[171] Notice whether or not there are large trees around the pool. If there are, ask about the leaf problem in the fall. In most cases, whatever is said, realize that falling leaves are one of the more difficult of pool pollutants to control and remove. The only effective preventive method is a sturdy diligently utilized pool cover. Because of normal human laziness after a day in the sun and water, pool covers have a way of not being put in place. An automatic cover is strongly recommended. All you have to do is press a button, and the job's done. The rule: Lots of big trees—with their bales of fall leaves—around the pool equals automatic pool cover.

[172] Healthy pool water *must* be blue. Some folks think that coloring the pool walls with blue pool paint will impart the desired fresh, clear, enticing blue color to the pool water. *Not true!* The bluest and cleanest pools have pure white Marbelite plaster walls. Clean, bacteria- and spore-free water, properly filtered, will be blue at any depth beyond three feet. The health department test for public pools is to toss a fifty-cent piece into the deep end. A person with normal eyesight should be able to determine whether it's heads or tails. In a home pool you should be able to manage the same test with a quarter. Clarity and the blue tint to pool water are essential to safety. Too many people have drowned in cloudy pools because onlookers couldn't see them clearly. Green pool water is polluted and unsafe for humans. The color indicates algae spores which support *B. coli* bacteria.

[173] Patches of green or black tar like stains on the pool walls and floor are the most common pool infections. The green algae is relatively easy to remove chemically. The black algae spores are nearly impossible to remove without shocking the water with such powerful herbicides that swimming must be forbidden for several days. These spores have been known to penetrate the walls to earth, through eight inches of reinforced, marble-plastered concrete. Shocking with copper sulfate (commercial bluestone), an active poison, or massive infusions of gaseous or liquid chlorine is the recommended shock treatment for this insidious growth. Of course, chlorine is an active poison as well, but it is normally used in mild-formula doses to keep the water clean and clear (blue). Other com-

mercial dry-chlorine and algaecidal preparations such as quaternary ammonium can also be utilized in removing this problem, but all of them are dangerous in the hands of untrained amateurs. The cost of professional removal of black algae is quite high, yet it is recommended.

[174] The pool filter system should be working when you arrive to inspect the property. This implies that the electricity is on in the house and everywhere else on the property. Pool water *must* be filtered and treated with algaecides in maintenance doses, on regular daily schedules. Most pool owners set their automatic time clocks for from six to eight hours of filter operation each day. If the filter isn't in service when you arrive, have it turned on so that you can check its effectiveness.

[175] Look at the skimmer. This device is identified by a round or rectangular cover, set behind the coping on the deck (figure 38). (Coping is

Figure 38.

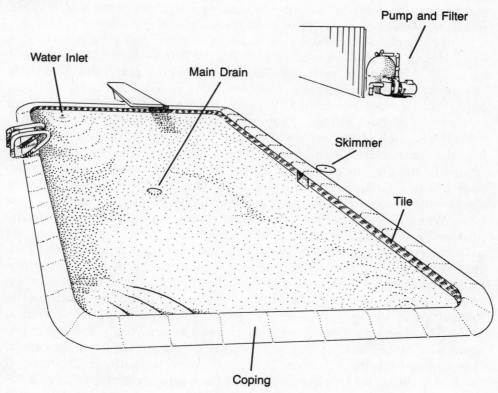

Typical Swimming Pool

the cast-concrete decorative stone around the top edge of the pool.) When you lift the skimmer lid you should see a basket, designed to catch leaves and other debris floating on the pool surface. Water should be active in the basket. Some skimmers are so active that they nearly vortex as they suck surface water and debris into the basket. If the action is lazy and the leaves just sort of undulate slowly in the chamber, the skimmer is ineffective. At this point, get down on your knees and look into the throat of the skimmer, where the water is coming in. You should see a kind of floating gate there, called the weir. The top edge of the weir lies just beneath the surface of the water when the skimmer is working properly. It is designed to keep the incoming water formed in a fast-moving sheet which sucks in the floating junk. Without a weir, the skimmer is all but useless. Other causes of slow skimmer action are a mismatched filter pump with inadequate suction, a plugged suction line, or a plugged skimmer discharge fitting. The only simple, owner-correctable cause of this problem is a fully packed skimmer basket. The remedy is simply to remove it and empty out the collected refuse. Any other cause requires professional attention.

[176] Now check the water inlet fittings. In most pools there are one or two holes in the shallow-end wall. With the filter running, there should be a nice, brisk water flow into the pool through those holes. One hole should produce a strong stream. Two holes will divide the total filter output into a more moderate flow from each location. Classier pools have chrome-plated inlet fittings. They aren't necessary, but they look nice.

[177] The main drain is very important (figure 39). Quite often you will find drains that are token chrome-plated grates over totally plugged-up sumps in the bottom of the pool. The main drain is the first swimming pool utility to deteriorate. The reason is that pools are heavy concrete shells which bear down on the pipe that runs from the pool bottom to the filter. When the pool is filled with water, more weight bears down on the pipe and fittings. Quite often, pool contractors don't realize that they are building on earth strata that may slip and shift. Pools have been constructed in ground that admits underground streams in the wintertime. Emptying the pool can cause it to float like a ship in such circumstances. In any case, movement of the pool bowl puts an incredible strain on the main-drain assembly. The only way to test the main-drain is to isolate it at the filter and let all the recirculation water be drawn through the main-drain line. Near the filter there are usually two or three filter inlet valves. One comes from the skimmer. A second comes from the main drain. If there is a third, it probably comes from a vacuum cleaner fitting in the pool wall. Most people don't use them anymore, so the third valve will probably be off.

Figure 39.   **Pool and Spa Equipment**

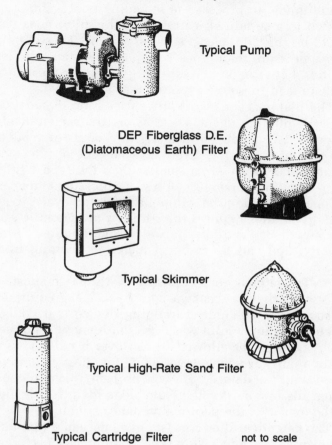

Typical Pump

DEP Fiberglass D.E.
(Diatomaceous Earth) Filter

Typical Skimmer

Typical High-Rate Sand Filter

Typical Cartridge Filter   not to scale

Turn off the skimmer valve and open the main drain valve all the way (counterclockwise, or turning to your left). If the filter continues to operate properly, and you feel water input at the inlets, the main drain is okay. If the filter pump begins to "starve" and rattle, and there is no inlet water, the main drain is no longer functional. Once enlightened, you shouldn't tolerate this condition. The cost of rehabilitation is massive. Failure to disclose a disabled swimming pool main drain before a sale could be actionable.

[178] Now that you're on speaking terms with the filter system (figure 39), let's have a good look at it. It usually consists of one large drumlike vessel, hooked up to a pump with a network of "face piping." There are three basic filter types:

111

Type 1: The rapid-sand filter uses specially selected sand, of uniform grain size and grade, to process the incoming pool water and remove all particles down to a certain size from it. If this filter does its job, it will keep the pool bright blue, clear, and very clean. These filters operate at slightly lower pressure than types 2 and 3. They can also usually go for longer periods between backwashings—the filter-cleaning process. I strongly recommend these over types 2 and 3 filters.

Type 2: The diatomaceous-earth filter uses filter elements coated with diatomite as the filtering agent. Diatoms are the skeletons of minute sea organisms deposited on the earth many thousands of years ago, and reclaimed by man as a filtering material. This type of filter will eliminate particles from water many sizes smaller than the type 1 filter, but it requires more attention, operates at higher pressures, demanding more pump horsepower, and quite often has shorter cycles between backwashes. This type filter requires the addition of diatomite each time it is flushed (backwashed). The filter tanks can be mounted either vertically or horizontally, and can be made of materials ranging from plastic to stainless steel.

IMPORTANT: Diatomaceous-earth filters discharge substantial quantities of solids when they are backwashed. It is a legal requirement in many areas that such filters include a trapping device that collects the used diatomite, along with all solid waste, so that they will not be discharged into the public sewers or allowed to run over a neighbor's land. These collectors are a fairly recent innovation. If the filter you are inspecting is not equipped with the device, you will probably have to install one soon after you take possession. If you are unable to identify this piece of equipment, ask the owner or the pool maintenance company.

Type 3: The cartridge filter consists of replaceable porous membranes or filter elements in a tank. This type of filter is most popular for spa installations. Now there are cartridge filters that are perfectly capable of filtering the larger swimming pools, but the cost of replacement elements, when the filters fill up with particles, is considerable. So far the best use for this type of filter is for spas, hot tubs, and very small pools. If you see such an installation on a large pool, be sure to ask the owner about the annual cost of replacement elements. Cartridge filters do not require backwashing and can be designed with either horizontal or vertical tanks.

[179] Look at the filter system and its environment carefully. Is the area surrounding the filter clean, organized, and uncluttered? Are the filter tank and pump, with its pipe network, organized in orderly patterns? Do you see any leaks between the pump motor and pump (usually one piece)? Check to see if there are drips coming down from any portion of the pump

motor assembly. Is the pipework leak-free? Do you see excessive amounts of water (puddling) in the vicinity? Does the pump hum smoothly? Any sharp gurgling or rattling within the pump could signal "cavitation," a condition where the pump is not getting enough water from the pool for its design. It is not a good condition and usually calls for costly professional remedies.

Check the filter system's valves. Make sure that they fully open and close easily. Sticky valves can be an aggravation.

Ask a few questions about the filter system. By all means get the name of the company or person who maintains or repairs it when it breaks down.

[180] Have someone demonstrate all of the filter functions, including:

1. Setting the filter for the normal filter cycle.
2. Setting the filter for backwash. If convenient, go through the backwash procedure.
3. Setting the filter for vacuuming. Ask for a demonstration.
4. Setting the system to empty the pool. The demonstration should consist of discharging a few gallons of water to illustrate the procedure.

If you are seriously interested in purchasing the property, the following demonstration would also improve your general knowledge of the pool's operation.

[181] Cleaning and chemical routines. Run through the whole pool operation schedule with the owner or service technician. Find out how often on average, the filter is backwashed or cartridge filter elements are replaced. What are the chemical additives and cleaning procedures? How do you test for chlorine residuals and the "pH factor"?

[182] Check the decks and coping for breaches and cracks. Cracked decks should be repaired quickly to prevent water from eroding the under-deck areas. The coping should be sound. Its grout (mortar) should be intact and form a good seal to the pool bond beam and the deck edge. (The bond beam is a massive concrete structure that binds together all of the pool's reinforcing steel. It's located under the coping.)

If everything checks out—the pool is clean, clear, and blue; the filter system runs efficiently and circulates the water at a brisk rate; the pool walls and bottom are free of algae; the decks and coping are sound and sealed; the equipment room or enclosure is neat, clean, reasonably dry, and well maintained; the skimmer works to its design capacity; and the bottom drain is in operating condition—then the pool meets all the tests of the NSPI (the National Swimming Pool Institute), and is a wonderful addition to the property. If it fails any of the important tests, a buyer should anticipate some expense in getting it up to standard. That expense can range from under a hundred dollars to several thousand dollars, depending upon the condition of the pool and its system.

IMPORTANT: Check to see if there are local ordinances or state laws requiring alarms, fences, and child-proof covers on swimming pools. In addition to statutory requirements, most insurance carriers require the installation of these safety features before they will write coverage on them.

The Spa

Spas—or hot tubs, as they are sometimes called—are becoming popular for a number of social reasons. For many, they are a substitute for a swimming pool. The premise is that they are less expensive initially, and they accomplish many similar objectives. They are a place to gather, relax, enjoy the pleasures of communication and the solidarity of community.

The only real expense after purchase is the cost of heating the water to temperatures over 100 degrees. Believe me, that's not a minor expense, so one of the things you'll want to look at critically is the spa heating system. Because spa and pool heaters are so similar (in most cases identical), I shall discuss that equipment as a separate item (see [185]).

[183] Spa types are separated into distinct categories. They range from very simple two-person barrels to complex and ornate Romanesque extravaganzas. Somewhere in the middle are the well-known and respected Jacuzzis about which most of us have heard. The high-end baths or tubs are usually so large and so similar in construction to small swimming pools that you would do well to apply the same criteria to them that I have suggested in the section on pools.

The most popular spa types are:

1: The reclaimed or imitation wine barrel with wooden seats and supports, with a design capacity of one to six persons.

2: The reinforced-fiberglass all-in-one-unit spa. This category includes tubs that have remote heaters and equipment, but the current preference is for the complete system to be built and installed as one unit. The usual design capacity ranges from one to eight persons.

3: The built-in masonry unit, with tile decor, including all the bells and whistles one could imagine, suitable for from one to ten or more persons. These are similar to type 4, but are considerably smaller and less ornate.

4: The Roman orgy. Please refer to "The Swimming Pool." These spas can be designed to accommodate twenty or more persons in unabashed luxury. Many are built in conjunction with regular swimming pools. Some even share equipment.

Here I'll cover types 1 and 2, the only ones that are significantly different from swimming pools.

[184] The wooden spa started it all. When one thinks of hot tubs, this type comes most readily to mind. These units usually stand on or are recessed into wooden decks. Wherever you have a lot of wood, you face the possibility of dry rot and termite infestation. The deck support structure follows the same rules as any other wooden framing or siding. It must be set on concrete, and stand at least six inches above the soil. The preferred material for the tub, decks, and supports is kiln-dried no. 1 finished-four-sides center-cut redwood. This is one of the most expensive woods you can imagine, but any other material has a somewhat shorter life span in service. Cedar (for decks), pine (for support structures), and oak (for tubs) have been used with some success, but the real answer is redwood.

Because you're dealing mainly with wood here, you must look upon the unit and its environment exactly as you would any other wooden structure. As I said before, look for rot and other infestations. If you detect them, you will have the problems (and expenses) of rehabilitation.

Those tubs constructed of reclaimed wine barrels should be more closely examined than the ones built as spas from scratch. Be sure that the staves are tight and holding water. One problem with this type is that when a house falls vacant pending sale, the average seller often doesn't treat a hot tub with the same consideration as a swimming pool, which must be kept under constant filtration and treatment. Quite often the spa is drained and left standing empty. In a few days the staves begin to dry out. In time, they shrink and loosen. When the new owner fills the spa and gets ready to enjoy the tub, water pours out the sides through the stave joints. It will take days and a lot of water to seal up the spa again. Sometimes it never recovers from the dry-out and requires professional resealing.

Built-from-scratch wooden hot tubs usually survive short-term dry-outs, but my experience has been that all wooden tubs suffer from this problem when they have been dry for more than a week in warm weather. They must be kept full.

[185] Unfortunately, if they are, another problem can develop. Stinking spa water is a direct result of neglect. It must be treated exactly as if it had happened in a swimming pool. Spa water must be treated for sanitation and algae control. The chemical of choice is usually chlorine in

one of its many forms. There is also the problem of human waste. The skin and hair discharge oils and particles into the spa. The fact that people are bathing at over 100 degrees in very active, swirling aerated water causes other body chemicals to be released. If there is no effective sanitation, the spa becomes a gigantic agar dish for breeding and suporting colonies of bacteria and algae spores. The telltale signs of problem spa water are slime deposits on the spa walls and noxious odors from its water.

[186] The one indispensable device required by every spa is the spa cover. It should be properly configured to seal the spa up completely. Without it, the spa will give up its retained heat to the atmosphere, increasing your heating bills. Leaves, pine needles, windblown trash, and little kids can fall into the tub. The consequences are obvious. The cover should be strong, completely intact, and a good fit. If you have children, it is recommended that you acquire the child-proof version rather than the floating type. Remember, a spa is considered an "attractive nuisance" under the law if neighbor children have access to it while you're away. If someone is injured or drowned in an owner's absence because the spa is not protected by fencing or other obstacles to easy entry by children, the owner can be held liable.

[187] The fiberglass spa is probably the easiest unit to service, maintain, and use. It often comes complete with its own electric heater, pump, and aeration system. Most of them include very effective spa covers, and skimmers much like swimming pool types, and are thermostatically protected. The only problem you should look for, unless the system has broken down and is not operating, is in the support structure and decking. Apply the same rules to those important items as I have suggested in [184] above.

The fiberglass spa needn't be kept full to remain watertight, a distinct advantage of this type over wooden tubs.

[188] The spa filter system is generally identical to swimming pool systems as indicated in [179] and [180] above. With few exceptions they are type 3 (cartridge-element) filters as delineated in [178]. Use the same inspection procedures as outlined in the appropriate swimming pool filter section. An exception to the general swimming pool pump/filter configuration is that hot tub filters seldom have more than one pump inlet. The one inlet should be valved.

[189] Fossil fuel swimming pool and spa heaters are usually confined to those burning either natural or liquified-petroleum gas. There are some oil burners and an occasional coal-fired heater, but they are so rare that I would suggest conversion or replacement wherever they are found. Maintenance and operating costs can be astronomical.

As for the gas burners, annual operating costs are only slightly less breathtaking. It takes an awful lot of heat to raise thirty or forty thousand gallons of swimming pool water one degree. On the other hand, the spa, with its smaller water volume, is a much more modest matter.

Whatever my opinion with respect to heating pool water with gas or any other fossil fuel, let me suggest that your concern is the operating efficiency of the heater in place at the time of your survey.

[190] Again, appearance is all-important. If the heater is clean and reasonably rust-free it's probably been relatively well maintained. There should be no holes in the vent stack. The pipework should be leak-free. When the controls are set and the filter pump turned on, the heater should ignite automatically. By all means, have someone demonstrate the ignition cycle. When the burner flame has been on for about five minutes, look into the burner sight-port or through the manifold opening in the sheet metal casing. The flame should be blue with occasional yellow flecks. If most of the flame is yellow, the air regulation shutters are poorly adjusted. That is an easy matter to cure, but it is an indication of carelessness and lack of attention to operating economy. Yellow flame makes soot. It could also be an indication of water vapor leakage into the firebox, the initial sign of potential tube system or jacket failure. If in doubt, suggest that the heater be checked by an expert. Replacement costs can run into four figures.

The ultimate indicator of an effective pool heater is whether or not it heats the water. You can check it at the pool inlets (see [176]). If the water coming in is substantially warmer than the surrounding pool water, the heater is doing its job. How efficiently it is doing its work is a matter for experts. It will also be measured by the size of the gas bill at the end of each month—a matter you probably want to discuss with the owner or seller anyway.

The water in a spa should heat from 60 degrees to over 100 degrees in less than five hours, depending on its water volume and the size of the heater. Most spa builders size heaters to accomplish the preceding heating task. If the job takes substantially more time, the heater is undersized.

[191] Solar pool heaters: Regardless of what you may or may not have heard about solar water heating, it is the most cost-effective means of heating pool and spa water. The initial investment is ordinarily the last if the system is properly designed and maintained.

Here again, it is best to get expert advice on the true condition of the system. I can, however, give you a few yardsticks by which to measure any solar system that's in place when you do your survey.

[192] The usual appearance and ''neatness'' injunctions apply. In the

case of swimming pool solar heaters, the piping is generally plastic (PVC—polyvinyl chloride), as are the fittings and many of the operating devices. This material seldom leaks. It is either good or bad from day one. If the leaks were removed at the time of installation, it is highly unlikely that some would have developed later, unless the owner decided to make a modification and didn't quite have his act together.

[193] Look the piping over carefully. Be especially cautious of any heavily taped or metal-banded surfaces. They could conceal puncture leaks or cracked pipe. Ask questions if and when you see something suspicious. Metal banding can also be part and parcel of the pipe assembly method in certain areas. Often you will find metal bands tightening against rubber or neoprene couplings. Those are fine.

[194] All exterior piping should be black. That is very important. White PVC that is perfectly acceptable for interior work *must* be painted black for use outdoors. Special black PVC is available for exterior installation. The ultraviolet rays from the sun can cause the white pipe to deteriorate quickly. White pipe on the outside should be painted immediately with black latex (water-base) paint.

[195] Swimming pool solar systems almost never have pumps of their own. Water is simply diverted through the solar system and is circulated by the main pool pump. Spas, on the other hand, usually have small pumps that are dedicated to circulating water through copper or PVC pipe to a heat exchanger during the sunny hours, as a *backup* for a gas heater. The spa's solar pump and heat exchanger bring the spa water up to temperature for pennies a day. Then the expensive gas heater operates only to maintain the temperature while the tub is in use. This combination can make a spa a rather inexpensive luxury.

[196] Solar collectors should face south or southwest for maximum effectiveness. In the absence of a south-facing roof, a completely level surface will do for pool and spa solar collectors. Be sure that any surface on which the collectors are mounted is open to the direct rays of the sun. A great many trees obstructing the sun's rays in its path from east to west can substantially reduce the solar heater's effectiveness.

[197] If in doubt, have all equipment demonstrated either by the owner or his representative.

8

Special Legal Checklist

This section covers some of the legal issues that can be involved in real estate transactions. It also gives you a list of questions—related to these legal issues—that you should try to answer before committing yourself to buying a property.

In most cases, you'll be asking the seller—or seller's representative or agent—these questions. Keep a good record of their responses for future reference.

Not all of the questions will apply to your situation—if some are irrelevant, simply omit them from your investigations. On the other hand, it's always better to be aware that these issues exist—and may be relevant—than to discover them through litigation. As legal problems, if they affect you, they are critical.

All of the items on this list have been tested or were being tested in the courts when this was written. Some of the issues, to be sure, are quasi-legalities (e.g., finding out whether a previous occupant was infected with a contagious disease). As an example of the way things are going, though, in one recent case a buyer sued when he discovered that a member of the seller's family had been infected with AIDS.

I haven't provided extensive explanations for these questions. You just need to know what kinds of problems have come up in previous transactions, and what areas of the law could be involved. If you detect a potentially serious legal problem—or an unanswered legal question—you should consult a lawyer.

YES NO N/A

[198] [ ] [ ] [ ] Is there anyone on the title who has not signed the listing agreement?

The reason for this question is obvious. All those on the title must receive consideration.

[199] [ ] [ ] [ ] Is there anyone on the title who is not a United States citizen?

Naturally, the IRS and the state and local tax folks want their share of any sale. There are currency restrictions on foreigners living abroad. Other legalities enter into this kind of transaction.

[200] [ ] [ ] [ ] Is there any divorce, bankruptcy, foreclosure, or the like that could impair the ability to transfer title?

This one is pretty much self-explanatory.

[201] [ ] [ ] [ ] Is the property currently under lease?

That lease could be a legal impediment to the transfer of clear title, depending on its provisions. On the other hand, you might be purchasing the property on the basis of such a lease.

[202] [ ] [ ] [ ] Does anyone have an option or right of first refusal to buy the property?

If such an option or right is a legally binding contract, the problem is obvious.

[203] [ ] [ ] [ ] Are there any encroachments, easements, boundary line disputes, or other claims by third parties affecting the property?

If there are, now is the time to get them out into the open.

[204] [ ] [ ] [ ] Have there been any additions or remodeling of any structure on the property?

This is the formal question. You have probably covered this item in your inspection, but it's important to have the question answered for the record.

[205] [ ] [ ] [ ] If so, were the necessary permits and government approvals obtained?

If they were, please ask to see them. If they are unavailable, check the appropriate government agencies for proof.

[206] [ ] [ ] [ ] Are you aware of any violations of state, local, or federal government laws affecting this property?

This is a straightforward question. In many cases the seller or agent might not know. Such violations can result in citations or liens being placed against the property by the governments involved. They may be so recent that the lien filings may not show up by the time of inquiry. Tax liens usually show up during the title search.

[207] [ ] [ ] [ ] Is there any existing, pending, or threatened legal action affecting the property?

The seller, mortgagee, trustee, or Deed of Trust beneficiary will usually have this information.

[208] [ ] [ ] [ ] Are there any unusual bonds or assessments affecting the property?

Such instruments as sewer bonds, water district assessments, and the like were alluded to earlier. This is the formal question.

[209] [ ] [ ] [ ] Is any loan on the property in default?

The seller must know.

[210] [ ] [ ] [ ] Is there any existing or pending IRS or other tax lien on the property?

This question appears to be a repeat of [206], but it is included because it specifically refers to liens, and is a backup. Of course, filed liens will be discovered during title search, but newly recorded and pending ones are quite another situation.

[211] [ ] [ ] [ ] Are there any existing or pending mechanics' liens on the property?

Often owners are not aware of mechanics' liens, which have been known to be filed by disgruntled or dishonest workmen, but the question should be asked for the record. The title search will do the rest.

[212] [ ] [ ] [ ] Has the property been surveyed, and when?

You will usually be referred to the government office in which the property records are filed. The seller should have the answer to this question. If it was surveyed before the current resident's occupancy, the records office is your only recourse.

[213] [ ] [ ] [ ] Are the property boundaries marked?

If the answer is yes, ask by what means the boundaries are marked: fence, stakes, landmarks, and so forth.

[214] [ ] [ ] [ ] Is the property in a special-studies zone as referred to in state or local law?

Special-studies zones can be set up by government to keep track of land movement, water incursion, various pollution problems, and toxic-waste control. Often neither the seller nor the buyer knows that such a zone exists. If there is no information forthcoming on that point, contact the EPA if you or any other parties to the transaction are suspicious.

[215] [ ] [ ] [ ] Is the property located in a designated flood zone?

Again, such a designation is the function of government agencies. This information is probably public knowledge. If you have suspicions, contact a local newspaper or an appropriate government agency.

The various types of "hazardous" zones can result in severe property insurance assessments and much higher premiums. Apart from that, there are certain construction requirements; e.g., wood shake or shingle roofs in fire hazard areas, beefed-up structural requirements in earthquake zones, and special foundation and grading requirements for flood zones. These all result in higher costs for structures of all kinds. Obviously, if you're looking for good construction at moderate cost, such areas should be avoided like the plague.

[216] [ ] [ ] [ ] Has the property ever had a drainage or flooding problem?

The seller should have the answer. If he doesn't, a nearby neighbor probably will. I've discussed this earlier in the manual. This question is for the record.

[217] [ ] [ ] [ ] Is the property located in a designated fire hazard zone?

Treat this question exactly as you did [215].

[218] [ ] [ ] [ ] Is the property located in a designated earthquake zone?

Again, see [215].

[219] [ ] [ ] [ ] Has the seller or any of his family recently been infected with a deadly infectious or incurable venereal disease?

Currently, AIDS is most people's biggest concern. Genital herpes is also a problem area, but most people overlook it. This is an extremely sensitive area of inquiry, and asking the question is strictly optional. You should ask your real estate agent to handle this one, if you are concerned. Current medical thinking holds that AIDS and other venereal infections cannot be spread by casual contact.

[220] [ ] [ ] [ ] Has there recently been a violent death or suicide on the property?

Often such an event will not faze a determined buyer, but you might be concerned as to whether such a history will affect your ability to resell the property later, especially if the property is located in a small town or rural area where such information can easily be picked up by prospective buyers.

[221] [ ] [ ] [ ] Are there any obvious neighborhood problems that could affect the enjoyment of the property by the buyer (e.g., high local crime rate, night drag racing in the streets, nearby fire station, etc.)?

This one is right to the point and deals with noise, nuisance, and security.

[222] [ ] [ ] [ ] Do you know if any urea-formaldehyde or asbestos materials were used in the construction of any structure on the property?

This question has similar connotations to the one on infectious diseases. It has to do with fear of bodily harm through illness caused by hazardous construction materials—which can be unseen and undisclosed pollutants.

Conclusions

After having inspected hundreds of homes during my career as a working plumber, electrician, and builder, and later as an inspector, I have come to realize that most of what I have been doing all my adult life is applying good old-fashioned common sense to what I've seen. Training as an inspector, surveyor, or appraiser is simply telling a person where to look, what to look for, and how to evaluate what is seen. Being able to utilize that simple training for proper assessments of rehabitation costs is a matter of applying that same common sense—which I have begun to discover isn't so common.

I have one hard, fast rule. "If it doesn't look and feel right, it probably isn't." When I run into a situation that arouses my suspicions, that's when I really get going. As I've said in the book, your eyes are almost always right, unless you have a medical problem with them. In fact, the human senses are usually correct in their perceptions. If the floor doesn't feel right. If the door looks just a bit out. If a pump motor rattles and makes other suspicious noises. If a porch rail sways in the hand. If a roof surface loses its clean line somewhere. If there are peculiar odors. If your questions are being answered evasively. If something zigs when you feel in your bones that it should zag. All of these "ifs" should be answered to your complete satisfaction—or you should pick up your marbles and look elsewhere.

If the owner says that something is in the process of being remedied or repaired, get it in writing and make it a part of the escrow conditions.

Pay absolutely no attention to complaints that you are being too fussy. When you're getting ready to pay a couple of hundred grand for a house, you have a perfect right to be fussy.

It goes without saying that you will probably not be able to complete the entire checklist when you go out to see a place, but reading the book will give you a set of important guidelines to consider. After you've been through a few listings from the local real estate broker, some of the principles will have become second nature to you—and you will have developed that instinctive inspector's skill that I call "nose."

The nose knows.

Good luck.

Bibliography

Fredriksson, Don. *Let Sol Do It, An Alternative Energy Guide*. Morrisville, Vt: Ark Press, 1986.

——*Plumbing for Dummies*. Indianapolis, Ind: Bobbs Merrill, 1983.

——*Residential Inspection Techniques*. Morrisville, Vt: Ark Press, 1986.

International Association of Plumbing and Mechanical Officials. *Uniform Mechanical Code*. Los Angeles, Calif: IAPMO, 1986.

——*Uniform Plumbing Code*. Los Angeles, Calif: IAPMO, 1986.

——*Uniform Solar Energy Code*. Los Angeles, Calif: IAPMO, 1986.

——*Uniform Swimming Pool, Spa and Hot Tub Code*. Los Angeles, Calif: IAPMO, 1986. International Conference of Building Officials. *Dwellings Constructed Under The Uniform Building Code*. Whittier, Calif: ICBO, 1984.

——*Uniform Building Code*. Whittier, Calif: ICBO, 1984.

Maloney, Roy T. *Real Estate Quick and Easy*. San Francisco, Calif: Drop Zone Press, 1986.

National Fire Protection Association. *National Electrical Code*. Quincy, Mass: NFPA, 1984.

Richter, H.P. and Schwan, W.C. *Wiring Simplified*. St. Paul, Minn: Park Publishing Inc., 1986.

Index